TO_My Shell_

FROM_SHEILA_

365 DAY BRIGHTENERS™

FINDING MY WAY

Inspiration for Teens

FINDING MY WAY
Inspiration for Teens

Copyright © 2005 DaySpring® Cards, Inc.
Published by Garborg's®,
a brand of DaySpring® Cards, Inc.
Siloam Springs, Arkansas 72761 www.dayspring.com

Design by Hot Dish Advertising, Minneapolis, MN

Quotes identified with a first name and last initial are from students representing churches from around the U.S. Due to age, their identities have been protected.

Scripture quotations are from the following sources: The HOLY BIBLE, NEW INTERNATIONAL VERSION® (NIV®) © 1973, 1978, 1984 by International Bible Society. Used by permission of Zondervan Publishing House. The Holy Bible, New Century Version (NCV) © 1987,1988, 1991 by Word Publishing, Dallas, Texas 75039. Used by permission. THE MESSAGE © Eugene H. Peterson 1993, 1994, 1995. Used by permission of NavPress Publishing Group. All rights reserved. The Living Bible (TLB) © 1971 by permission of Tyndale House Publishers, Inc., Wheaton, IL. The Holy Bible, New Living Translation (NLT) © 1996 by permission of Tyndale House Publishers, Inc., Wheaton, IL. The NEW AMERICAN STANDARD BIBLE® (NASB) © The Lockman Foundation 1960, 1962, 1963, 1968, 1971, 1972, 1973, 1975, 1977, 1995. Used by permission. (www.Lockman.org). The New Revised Standard Version of the Bible (NRSV) © 1989 Division of Christian Education, National Council of Churches. Used by permission of Zondervan Publishing House.
All rights reserved.

ISBN 1-59449-150-X
Printed in China

365 DAY BRIGHTENERS™

FINDING MY WAY

Inspiration for Teens

GARBORG'S®

because every day is a gift

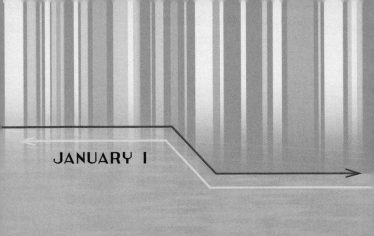

JANUARY 1

Every day is a new start.

DOUG M.

You made my whole being; you formed me in my mother's body. I praise you because you made me in an amazing and wonderful way. What you have done is wonderful. I know this very well. You saw my bones being formed as I took shape in my mother's body. When I was put together there, you saw my body as it was formed. All the days planned for me were written in your book before I was one day old.

PSALM 139:13-16 NCV

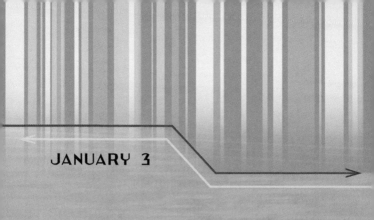

JANUARY 3

God is more interested in making us what we ought to be than in giving us what we think we ought to have.

JANUARY 4

I've learned that words hurt more than anything.

ZACH C.

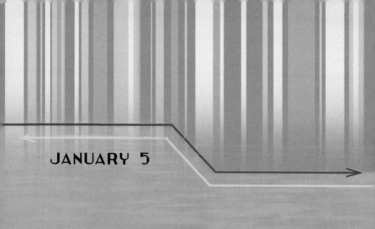

JANUARY 5

Form good habits. They are as hard to break as bad ones!

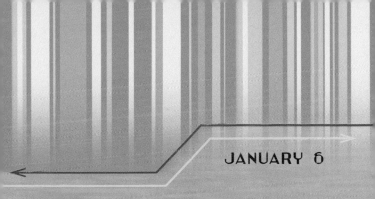

JANUARY 6

What you spend years building, someone could destroy overnight; Build anyway. If you find serenity and happiness, they may be jealous; Be happy anyway.… You see, in the final analysis, it is between you and God.

MOTHER TERESA

JANUARY 7

But I say, love your enemies! Pray for those who persecute you! In that way, you will be acting as true children of your Father in heaven. For he gives his sunlight to both the evil and the good, and he sends rain on the just and on the unjust, too.

MATTHEW 5:44-45 NLT

We do not understand the intricate pattern of the stars in their courses, but we know that He who created them does, and that just as surely as He guides them, He is charting a safe course for us.

BILLY GRAHAM

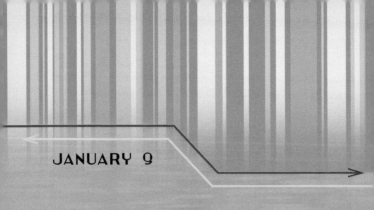

JANUARY 9

Live. Love and cherish life. Make friends, memories, and plans. Your life is about you, but life is not about you.

EMILY CAMPAGNA

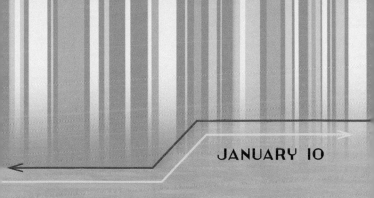

Don't give up. You can't know the outcome
until you finish.

DAVID M.

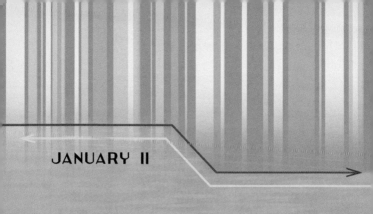

JANUARY II

Still round the corner there may wait,
a new road, or a secret gate.

J. R. R. TOLKIEN

Present your bodies as a living sacrifice, holy and acceptable to God, which is your spiritual worship. Do not be conformed to this world, but be transformed by the renewing of your minds, so that you may discern what is the will of God—what is good and acceptable and perfect.

ROMANS 12:1-2 NRSV

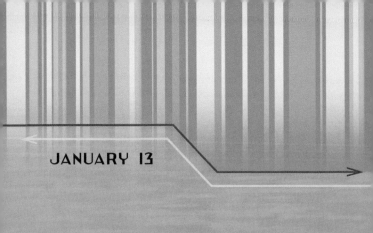

JANUARY 13

Don't focus on the don'ts. Focus on the dos.

STEPHANIE J.

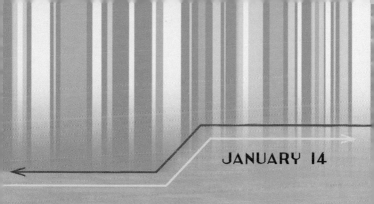

JANUARY 14

Let your religion be less of a theory and more
of a love affair.

G. K. CHESTERTON

JANUARY 15

Two roads diverged in a wood, and I—
I took the one less traveled by,
And that has made all the difference.

ROBERT FROST

JANUARY 16

First it is necessary to stand on your own two feet. But the minute you find yourself in that position, the next thing you should do is reach out your arms for a friend.

KRISTIN HUNTER LATTANY

JANUARY 17

I have told you these things, so that in me you may have peace. In this world you will have trouble. But take heart! I have overcome the world.

JOHN 16:33 NIV

The glory of friendship is found in the inspiration that comes when I discover that someone else believes in me and is willing to trust me with their friendship.

MARTIN LUTHER KING JR.

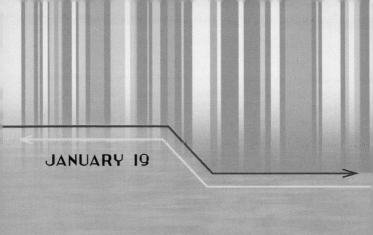

JANUARY 19

Praying works.... God is real!

SHELBY A.

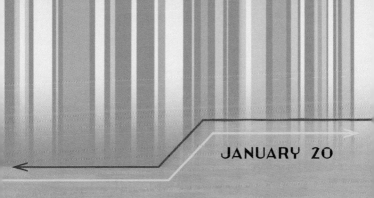

JANUARY 20

The good for which we are born into this world
is that we may learn to love.

GEORGE MACDONALD

JANUARY 21

The butterfly can just look back,
Flap those wings and say, "Oh, yeah!
I never have to be a worm again!"

SARA GROVES

No one is too young for God to speak to or to use.

PATTY R.

Don't let anyone look down on you because you are young, but set an example for the believers in speech, in life, in love, in faith and in purity.

1 TIMOTHY 4:12 NIV

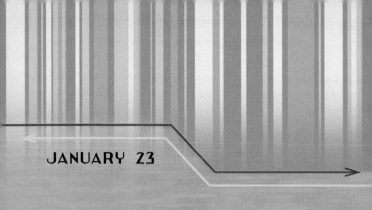

JANUARY 23

Joy comes from knowing God loves me and knows who I am and where I'm going...that my future is secure as I rest in Him.

JAMES DOBSON

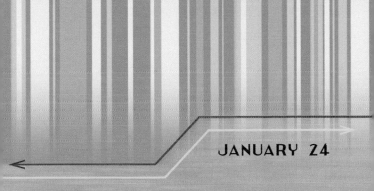

You must give some time to your fellow men.
Even if it's a little thing, do something for
others—something for which you get no pay
but the privilege of doing it.

ALBERT SCHWEITZER

JANUARY 25

You are not an accident. Your birth was no mistake or mishap, and your life is no fluke of nature. Your parents may not have planned you, but God did. He was not at all surprised by your birth. In fact, He expected it.

RICK WARREN

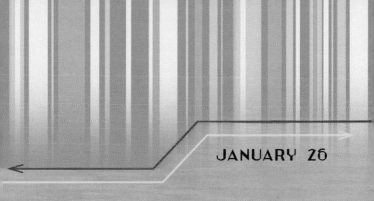

JANUARY 26

The riches that are in the heart cannot be stolen.

RUSSIAN PROVERB

JANUARY 27

For I can do everything with the help of Christ who gives me the strength I need.

PHILIPPIANS 4:13 NLT

No one has ever risen to the real stature of spiritual adulthood until one has found that it is finer to serve somebody else than it is to serve oneself.

WOODROW WILSON

Clear your mind of can't.

SAMUEL JOHNSON

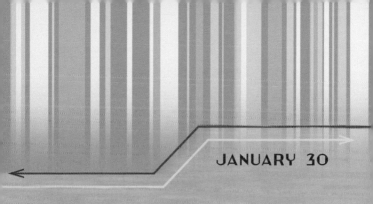

JANUARY 30

W hat God sends is better than what we ask for.

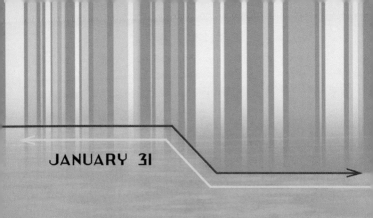

JANUARY 31

A good example has twice the value
of good advice.

Through thick and thin, keep your hearts at attention, in adoration before Christ, your Master. Be ready to speak up and tell anyone who asks why you're living the way you are, and always with the utmost courtesy.

1 PETER 3:15 THE MESSAGE

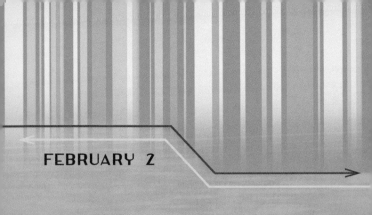

FEBRUARY 2

God loves you and made you exactly the way
He wanted. He has a plan for you.

KATE P.

FEBRUARY 3

Each day can be the beginning of a wonderful future.

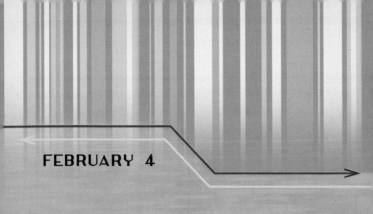

Whatever God tells us to do, He also helps us to do.

DORA GREENWELL

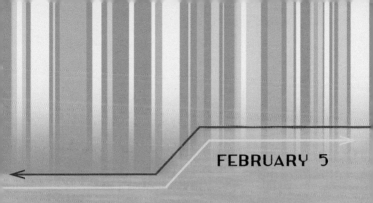

FEBRUARY 5

It isn't what happens: it's how you deal with it that's important.

FEBRUARY 6

Lord, when was it that we saw you hungry and gave you food, or thirsty and gave you something to drink?.... And the king will answer them, "Truly I tell you, just as you did it to one of the least of these who are members of my family, you did it to me."

MATTHEW 25:37, 40 NRSV

FEBRUARY 7

It is curious, but if one smiles, darkness fades.

BEATRICE WOOD

FEBRUARY 8

Either do not attempt at all, or go through with it.

OVID

FEBRUARY 9

When you're with someone you trust in,
never needing to pretend,
Someone who helps you know yourself...
you know you're with a friend.

AMANDA BRADLEY

FEBRUARY 10

Nothing is particularly hard if you divide it into small jobs.

HENRY FORD

Surprise us with love at daybreak; then we'll skip and dance all the day long.... And let the loveliness of our Lord, our God, rest on us, confirming the work that we do. Oh, yes. Affirm the work that we do!

PSALM 90:14, 17 THE MESSAGE

FEBRUARY 12

There is always hope. Even though sometimes it gets worse before it gets better, it does get better.

BEN B.

FEBRUARY 13

Friends are an indispensable part of a
meaningful life. They are the ones who share
our burdens and multiply our blessings.

BEVERLY LAHAYE

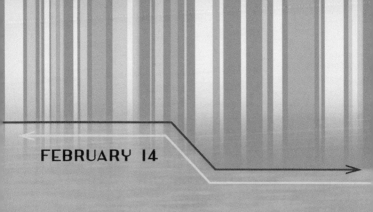

FEBRUARY 14

Giving encouragement to others is a most welcome gift, for the results of it are lifted spirits, increased self-worth, and a hopeful future.

FLORENCE LITTAUER

FEBRUARY 15

Better to try something and fail than to try nothing and succeed.

FEBRUARY 16

The father instantly replied, "I do believe, but help me not to doubt!"

MARK 9:24 NLT

FEBRUARY 17

Start by doing what's necessary, then what's possible, and suddenly you are doing the impossible.

FRANCIS OF ASSISI

FEBRUARY 18

Doing little things with a strong desire to please God makes them really great.

FRANCIS DE SALES

FEBRUARY 19

Don't let anyone pressure you into something you don't want to do.

LAITH A.

FEBRUARY 20

Friends remind us we are part of something greater than ourselves, a larger world, and the right friends keep us on track.

BARBARA JENKINS

Dear young friends, you belong to God and have already won your fight with those who are against Christ because there is someone in your hearts who is stronger than any evil.

1 JOHN 4:4 TLB

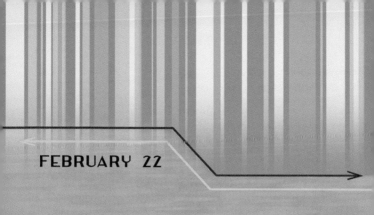

FEBRUARY 22

An amazing thing happens when we offer praise and thanksgiving to God. When we give God enjoyment, our own hearts are filled with joy!

RICK WARREN

FEBRUARY 23

Contentment is not the fulfillment of what you want, but the realization of how much you already have.

FEBRUARY 24

God's delays are not God's denials.

ROBERT SCHULLER

FEBRUARY 25

Courage means you are the only one who
knows you're afraid.

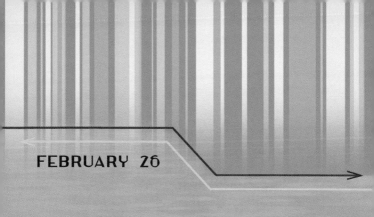

FEBRUARY 26

Let us continually offer to God a sacrifice of praise—the fruit of lips that confess his name. And do not forget to do good and to share with others, for with such sacrifices God is pleased.

HEBREWS 13:15-16 NIV

FEBRUARY 27

You never know whose life you're touching.

God does not ask your ability or your inability.
He asks only your availability.

MARY KAY ASH

FEBRUARY 29

The everyday choices you make depend
on your faith

RACHEL K.

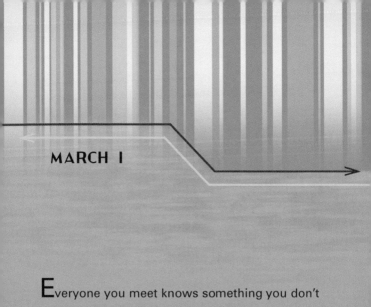

MARCH 1

Everyone you meet knows something you don't
know. Be willing to learn from them.

Instead, be really glad—because these trials will make you partners with Christ in his suffering, and afterwards you will have the wonderful joy of sharing his glory in that coming day when it will be displayed.

1 PETER 4:13 TLB

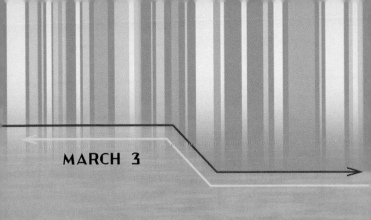

MARCH 3

Regardless of your past, your future is a clean slate.

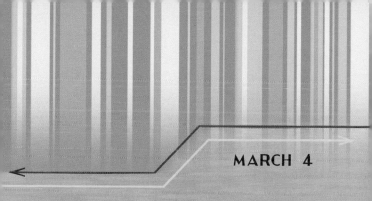

MARCH 4

If you wait for perfect conditions you will never get anything done.

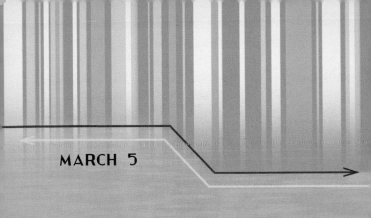

MARCH 5

God has a thousand ways
Where I can see not one;
When all my means have reached their end
Then His have just begun.

ESTHER GUYOT

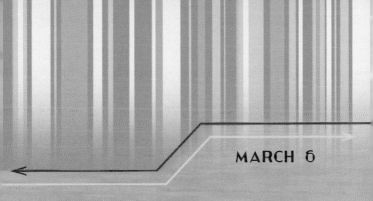

MARCH 6

How you do something and the attitude with which you do it are usually even more important than what you do.... Often we have no choice about doing things, but we can always choose how to do them. And that...can make all the difference.

NORMAN VINCENT PEALE

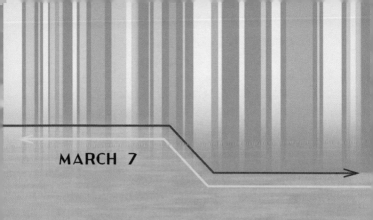

MARCH 7

Help me abandon my shameful ways; your laws
are all I want in life.

PSALM 119:39 NLT

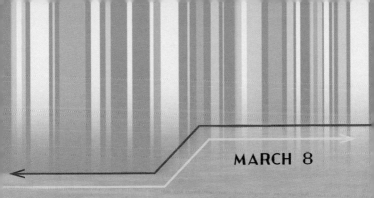

MARCH 8

Praying is important because it causes miracles.

CHRISTOPHER B.

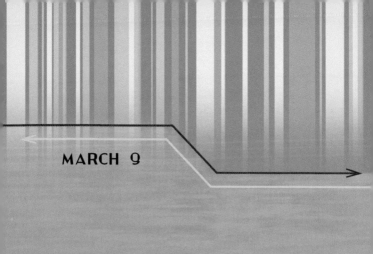

MARCH 9

Trust your friends with both the delightful and the difficult parts of your life.

LUCI SHAW

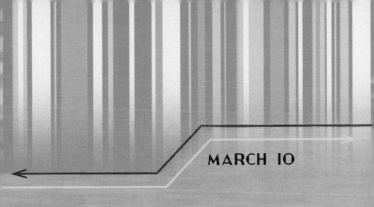

MARCH 10

It is often just as sacred to laugh as it is to pray.

CHARLES SWINDOLL

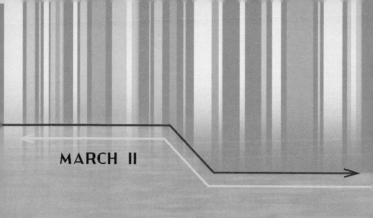

Tuck [this] thought into your heart today.
Treasure it. Your Father God cares about your
daily everythings that concern you.

KAY ARTHUR

But remember that the temptations that come into your life are no different from what others experience. And God is faithful. He will keep the temptation from becoming so strong that you can't stand up against it. When you are tempted, he will show you a way out so that you will not give in to it.

1 CORINTHIANS 10:13 NLT

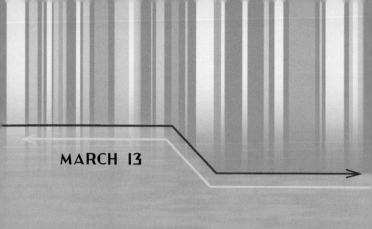

MARCH 13

None of us are responsible for our birth.
Our responsibility is the use we make of life.

JOSHUA HENRY JONES

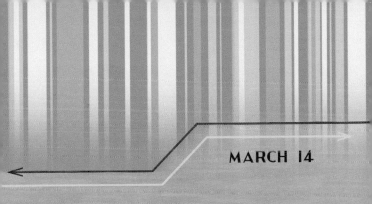

MARCH 14

I can't just know it, I've got to feel it.
And I can't just feel it, I've got to believe it.
And I can't just believe it, I've got to live it.

SARA GROVES

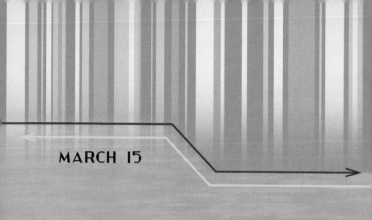

MARCH 15

Find the good. It's all around you. Find it, showcase it, and you'll start believing in it.

JESSE OWENS

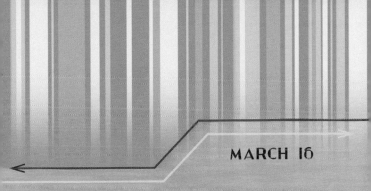

If it feels wrong—it is.

JESSIE N.

But if people have doubts about whether they should eat something, they shouldn't eat it. They would be condemned for not acting in faith before God. If you do anything you believe is not right, you are sinning.

ROMANS 14:23 NLT

MARCH 17

God's help is nearer than the door.

IRISH PROVERB

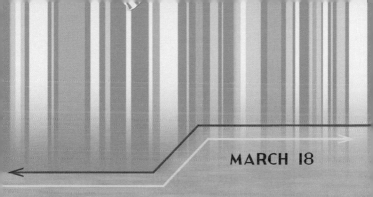

But God has promised strength for the day,
Rest for the labor, light for the way,
Grace for the trials, help from above,
Unfailing sympathy, undying love.

ANNIE JOHNSON FLINT

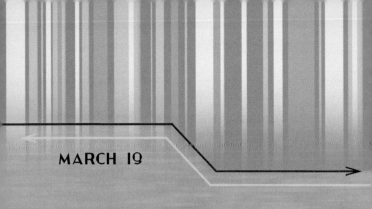

The good you do today, people will often forget tomorrow; Do good anyway. Give the world the best you have, and it may never be enough; Give the world the best you've got anyway.

MOTHER TERESA

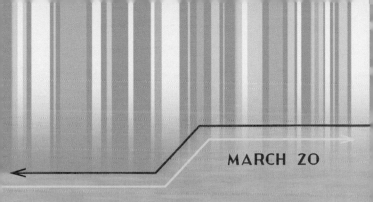

MARCH 20

There is no joy in life like the joy of sharing.

BILLY GRAHAM

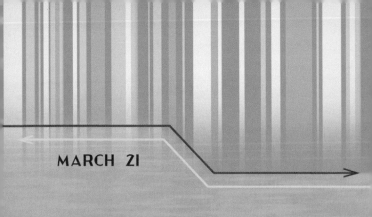

MARCH 21

Υou have to give yourself a place to start
and then dream big—that's the only way to get
where you want to go.

KRISTI H.

MARCH 22

Therefore put on the full armor of God, so that when the day of evil comes, you may be able to stand your ground, and after you have done everything, to stand.

EPHESIANS 6:13 NIV

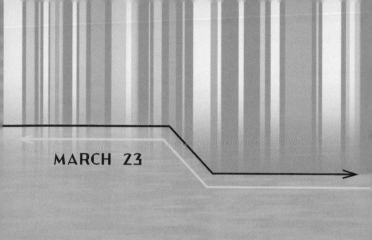

MARCH 23

A grudge is too heavy a load for anyone to carry.

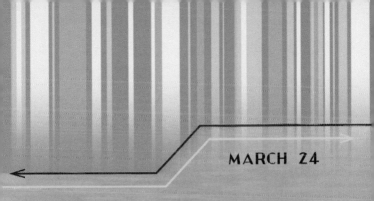

MARCH 24

God shall be my hope, my stay, my guide
and lantern to my feet.

SHAKESPEARE

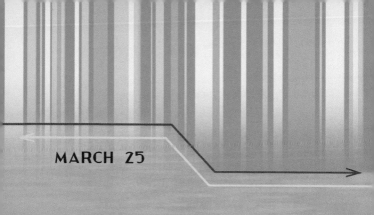

MARCH 25

You should shoot for your dreams and if you
miss you will still be better off than you were
before you tried.

CASSIE H.

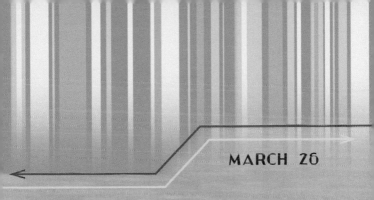

MARCH 26

There is something basic about friendship.
It is like the structure that holds up a building.
It is mostly hidden and absolutely essential.

EMILIE BARNES

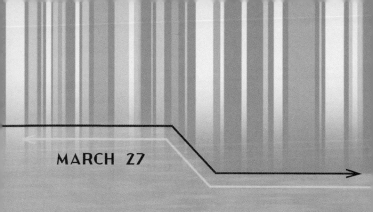

MARCH 27

For his Holy Spirit speaks to us deep in our hearts and tells us that we really are God's children. And since we are his children, we will share his treasures—for all God gives to his Son Jesus is now ours too.

ROMANS 8:16-17 TLB

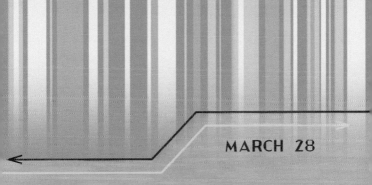

I expect to pass through life but once.
If therefore, there can be any kindness I can
show, or any good thing I can do to any fellow
being, let me do it now...as I shall not pass this
way again.

WILLIAM PENN

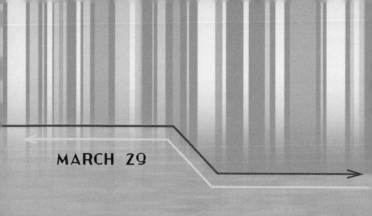

We should look for reasons to celebrate—
an A on a paper—even a good hair day.

PAM FARREL

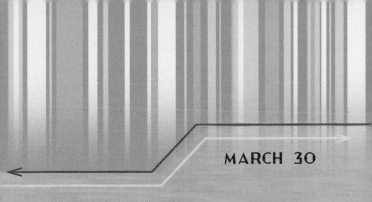

God makes our lives a medley of joy and tears,
hope and help, love and encouragement.

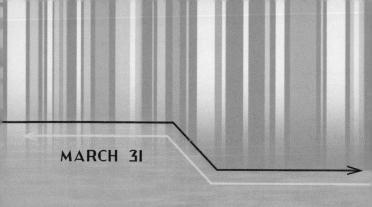

MARCH 31

Are not five sparrows sold for two pennies? Yet not one of them is forgotten in God's sight. But even the hairs of your head are all counted. Do not be afraid; you are of more value than many sparrows.

LUKE 12:6-7 NRSV

APRIL 1

Better to remain silent and be thought a fool
than to speak out and remove all doubt.

ABRAHAM LINCOLN

APRIL 2

God said He'd fulfill the dreams and desires
of my heart, so they must mean something.

MAGGIE T.

I don't know what the future holds, but I know who holds the future.

E. STANLEY JONES

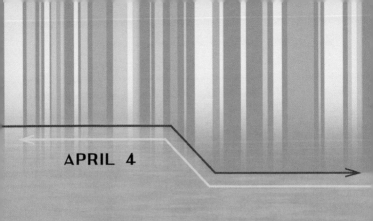

APRIL 4

Blessed are they who have the gift of making friends, for it is one of God's best gifts.

THOMAS HUGHES

We read more deeply, remember more clearly, enjoy events with greater pleasure if we have a friend to share with.

PAM BROWN

APRIL 6

Keep alert and pray. Otherwise temptation will overpower you. For though the spirit is willing enough, the body is weak!

MATTHEW 26:41 NLT

Reading the Bible helps you come up with
solutions to your problems.

DANIELLE I.

APRIL 8

I look to the future, because that's where I'm going
to spend the rest of my life.

GEORGE BURNS

Lord, when I am wrong, make me willing to change, and when I am right...make me easy to live with.

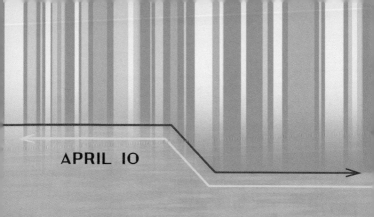

APRIL 10

It's the everyday miracles that keep my hope alive.
It's the way You move in little things that help
me survive.

SARA GROVES

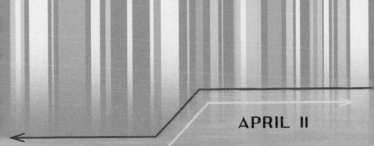

APRIL 11

I lift up my eyes to the hills—from where will my help come? My help comes from the Lord, who made heaven and earth…. He…will neither slumber nor sleep.

PSALM 121:1-2, 4 NRSV

APRIL 12

What is popular is not always right. What is right is not always popular.

NATHAN D.

APRIL 13

Indeed, we do not really live unless we have friends surrounding us like a firm wall against the winds of the world.

CHARLES HANSON TOWNE

APRIL 14

God has designs on our future…and He has designed us for the future. He has given us something to do in the future that no one else can do.

RUTH SENTER

APRIL 15

You will reach your destination if you walk
with God.

APRIL 16

Do not worry about your life, what you will eat or drink; or about your body, what you will wear. Is not life more important than food, and the body more important than clothes? Look at the birds of the air; they do not sow or reap or store away in barns, and yet your heavenly Father feeds them. Are you not much more valuable than they?

MATTHEW 6:25-26 NIV

APRIL 17

There is much satisfaction in work well done; praise is sweet, but there can be no happiness equal to the joy of finding a heart that understands.

VICTOR ROBINSON

APRIL 18

Admit your errors before someone else exaggerates them.

APRIL 19

F ew delights can equal the mere presence of one whom we trust utterly.

GEORGE MACDONALD

APRIL 20

Every day is a new day. Don't sweat the small stuff.

RYAN S.

APRIL 21

O Lord my God, you have done many miracles
for us. Your plans for us are too numerous to list.
If I tried to recite all your wonderful deeds,
I would never come to the end of them.

PSALM 40:5 NLT

APRIL 22

Every person's life is a fairy tale written by God's fingers.

HANS CHRISTIAN ANDERSEN

APRIL 23

As important as "hanging on," is knowing when to "let go."

SHERRI DEWITT

APRIL 24

Remember you are very special to God as His precious child. He has promised to complete the good work He has begun in you. As you continue to grow in Him, He will teach you to be a blessing to others.

GARY SMALLEY AND JOHN TRENT

APRIL 25

It may be a good thing to be rich, and a good thing to be strong, but it is a better thing to be loved of many friends.

APRIL 26

Listen to counsel and accept discipline, that you may be wise the rest of your days.

PROVERBS 19:20 NASB

APRIL 27

One loses so many laughs by not laughing at oneself.

SARA JEANNETTE DUNCAN

APRIL 28

Memories are treasures that we can enjoy again and again.

APRIL 29

Having it all doesn't necessarily mean having it all at once.

STEPHANIE LUETKEHAUS

APRIL 30

Miracles happen to those who believe in them.

BERNARD BERENSON

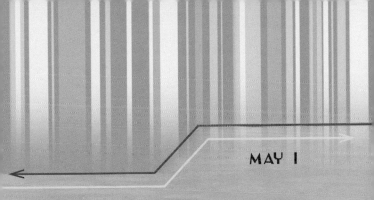

MAY 1

For the eyes of the Lord search back and forth
across the whole earth, looking for people whose
hearts are perfect toward him, so that he can
show his great power in helping them.

2 CHRONICLES 16:9 TLB

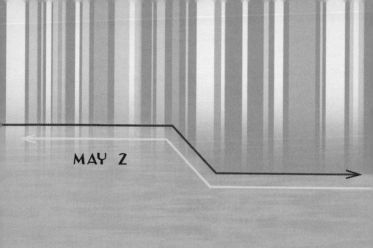

MAY 2

God is listening. Talk.

AMANDA B.

God's training is for right now, not for some mist-shrouded future. His purpose is for this minute, not for something better down the road. His power and His presence are available to you as you draw your next breath, not for some great impending struggle. This moment is the future for which you've been preparing!

JONI EARECKSON TADA

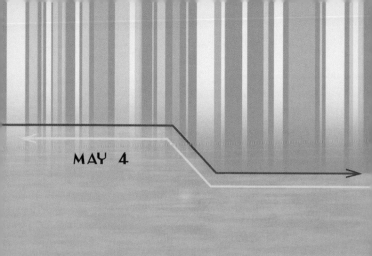

MAY 4

Success is getting what you want; happiness
is wanting what you get.

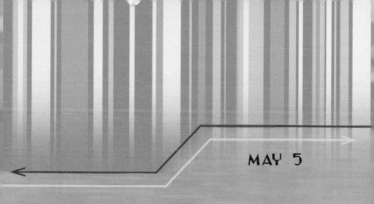

MAY 5

Each day brings us a chance to do better and to make good. It is as though our slate has had the smudges of yesterday wiped out.

L. BEVAN JONES

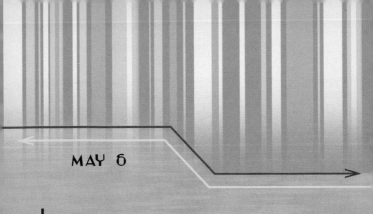

MAY 6

I know when I fall...I need Him to help me fly.

CHRISTIN R.

And he is able to keep you from slipping and
falling away, and to bring you, sinless and perfect,
into his glorious presence with mighty shouts
of everlasting joy.

JUDE 1:24-25 TLB

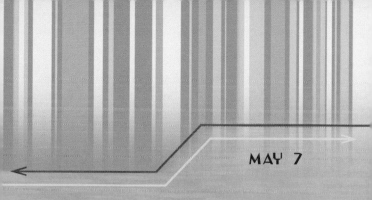

MAY 7

As God's workmanship, we deserve to be
treated, and to treat ourselves, with affection
and affirmation, regardless of our appearance
or performance.

MARY ANN MAYO

MAY 8

Laughter is the shortest distance between
two people.

VICTOR BORGE

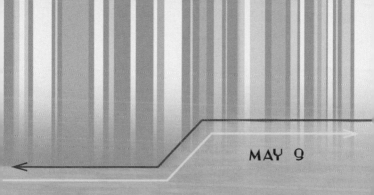

MAY 9

Maybe we could spend a moment at the end of each day and decide to remember that day—whatever may have happened—as a day to be grateful for. In so doing we increase our heart's capacity to choose joy.

HENRI J. M. NOUWEN

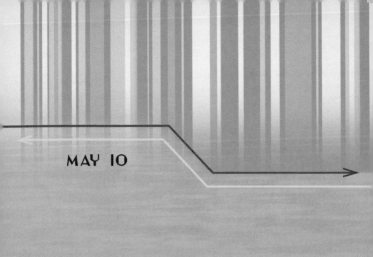

MAY 10

When hands reach out in friendship, hearts are touched with joy.

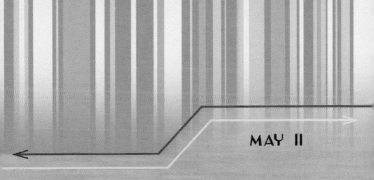

MAY 11

But that is why God had mercy on me, so that Christ Jesus could use me as a prime example of his great patience with even the worst sinners. Then others will realize that they, too, can believe in him and receive eternal life.

1 TIMOTHY 1:16 NLT

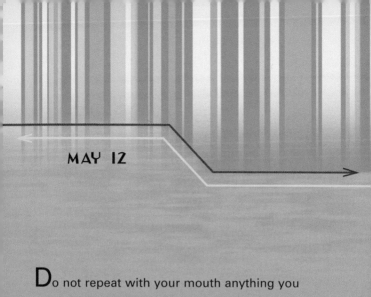

MAY 12

Do not repeat with your mouth anything you would not sign your name to for all the world to see.

MAY 13

There are no shortcuts to maturity. It takes years for us to grow to adulthood, and it takes a full season for fruit to mature and ripen. The same is true for the fruit of the Spirit. The development of Christlike character cannot be rushed.

RICK WARREN

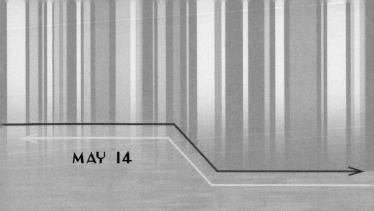

MAY 14

Allow your dreams a place in your prayers
and plans. God-given dreams can help you move
into the future He is preparing for you.

BARBARA JOHNSON

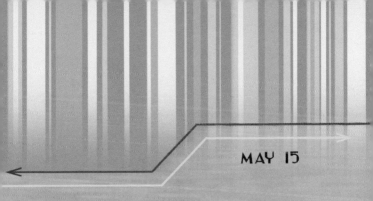

MAY 15

You have struggled to get where you are. If you give up now, you'll have wasted all your effort.

DANIEL B.

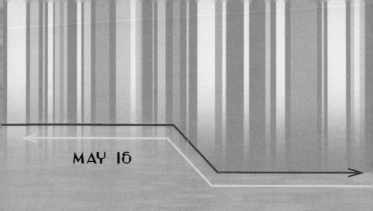

MAY 16

Let us not become weary in doing good, for at the proper time we will reap a harvest if we do not give up. Therefore, as we have opportunity, let us do good to all people.

GALATIANS 6:9-10 NIV

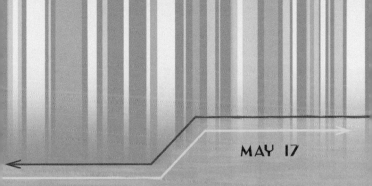

MAY 17

God is doing a work in me.
He's walking through my rooms and halls,
Checking every corner,
Tearing down the unsafe walls
And letting in the light.

SARA GROVES

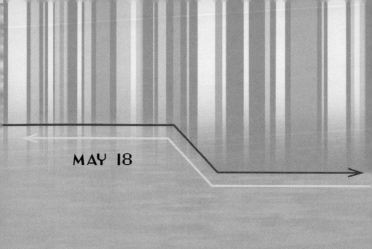

One of the secrets of a long and fruitful life is to forgive everybody everything, every night before you go to bed.

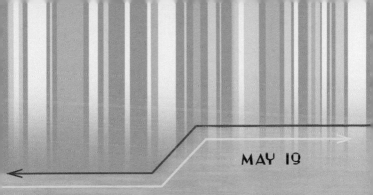

MAY 19

Some blessings—like rainbows after rain or a friend's listening ear—are extraordinary gifts waiting to be discovered in an ordinary day.

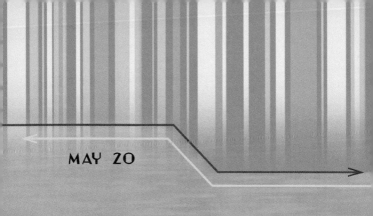

MAY 20

We are most of us very lonely in this world;
you who have any who love you, cling to them
and thank God.

WILLIAM MAKEPEACE THACKERAY

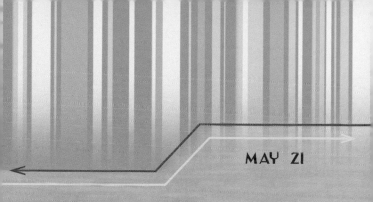

MAY 21

I think it is better to inform people about faith with action more than with words.

DAN P.

My children, we should love people not only with words and talk, but by our actions and true caring.

1 JOHN 3:18 NCV

MAY 22

The most wasted of all our days are those in which we have not laughed.

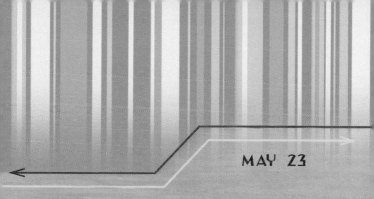

MAY 23

Spring is God's way of saying, "One more time!"

ROBERT ORBEN

MAY 24

There's always something for which to be thankful.

CHARLES DICKENS

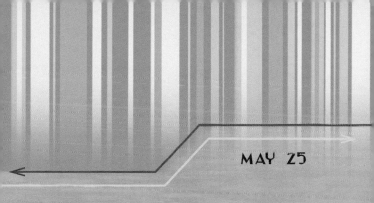

MAY 25

God loves each one of us as if there were only one of us.

AUGUSTINE

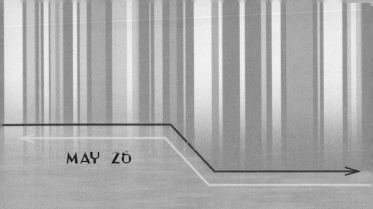

MAY 26

You did not choose Me, but I chose you, and appointed you, that you should go and bear fruit, and that your fruit should remain, that whatever you ask of the Father in My name, He may give to you.

JOHN 15:16 NASB

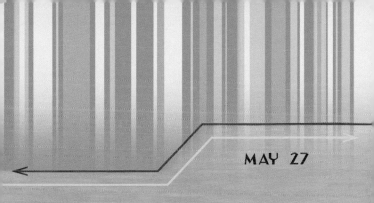

MAY 27

The princes among us are those who forget themselves and serve mankind.

WOODROW WILSON

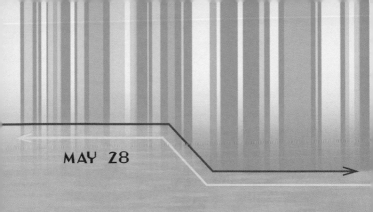

MAY 28

Love keeps on growing through life's joys and tears, bringing a fragrance that sweetens with years.

ROY LESSIN

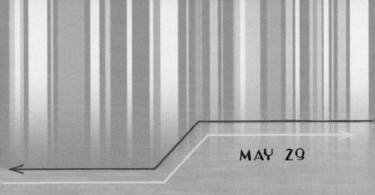

MAY 29

Politeness is a trait in folks
That's easy to explain;
They're the first to show their gratitude,
And the last ones to complain.

CARICE WILLIAMS

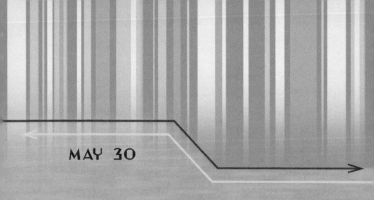

MAY 30

Whenever we realize we have not taken advantage of a magnificent opportunity, we are apt to sink into despair. Let the past sleep, but let it sleep in the sweet embrace of Christ, and let us go on into the invincible future with Him. Never let the sense of past failure defeat your next step.

OSWALD CHAMBER

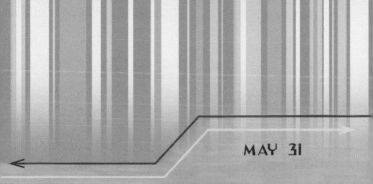

MAY 31

Find common ground.

STEVE H.

Finally, all of you, live in harmony with one another; be sympathetic, love as brothers, be compassionate and humble. Do not repay evil with evil or insult with insult, but with blessing, because to this you were called so that you may inherit a blessing.

1 PETER 3:8-9 NIV

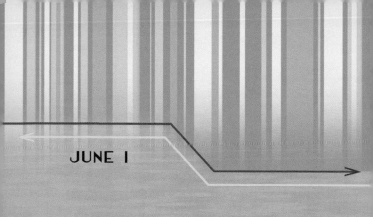

JUNE 1

Never be afraid to trust an unknown future to an all-knowing God.

CORRIE TEN BOOM

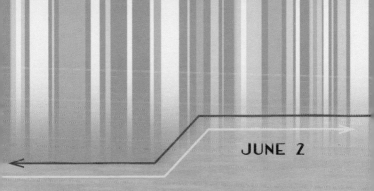

JUNE 2

Try to put into practice what you already know;
and in so doing, you will, in good time, discover
the hidden things which you now inquire about.
Practice what you know, and it will help to make
clear what you do not know.

REMBRANDT

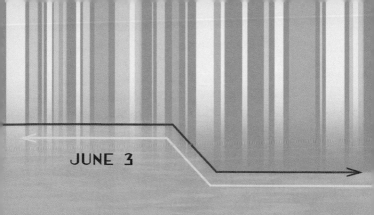

JUNE 3

God created the world out of nothing, and so
long as we are nothing, He can make something
out of us.

MARTIN LUTHER

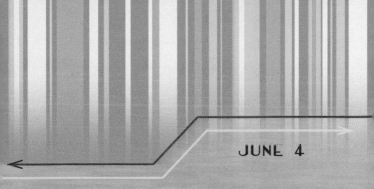

Today the average life span is 25,550 days.
That's how long you will live if you are typical.
Don't you think it would be a wise use of time to
set aside [some] of those days to figure out what
God wants you to do with the rest of them?

RICK WARREN

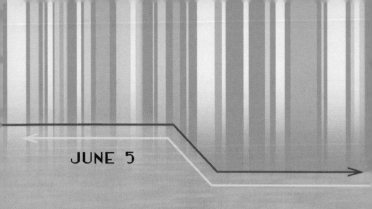

JUNE 5

Take your everyday, ordinary life—your sleeping, eating, going-to-work, and walking-around life— and place it before God as an offering. Embracing what God does for you is the best thing you can do for him.

ROMANS 12:1 THE MESSAGE

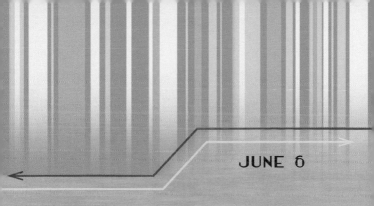

JUNE 6

You shouldn't see how close you can get to sin without doing it, but how far away you can run from it.

ISAAC B.

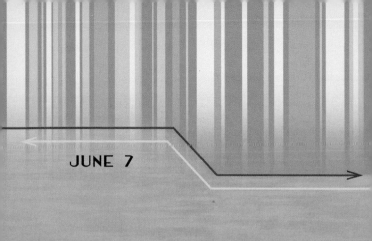

JUNE 7

God's hand is always there; once you grasp it you'll never want to let it go.

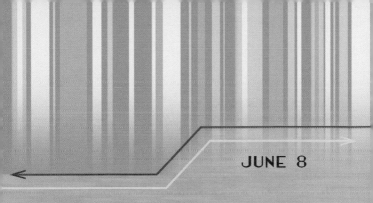

Wise people, even though all laws were abolished, would still lead the same life.

ARISTOPHANES

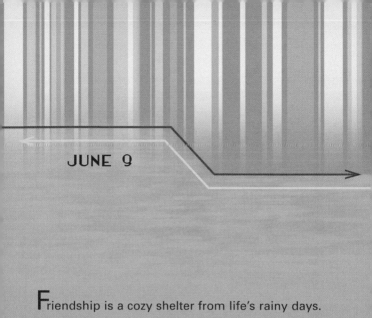

JUNE 9

Friendship is a cozy shelter from life's rainy days.

JUNE 10

I entreat you to walk in a manner worthy of the
calling with which you have been called, with all
humility and gentleness, with patience, showing
forbearance to one another in love, being
diligent to preserve the unity of the Spirit in
the bond of peace.

EPHESIANS 4:1-3 NASB

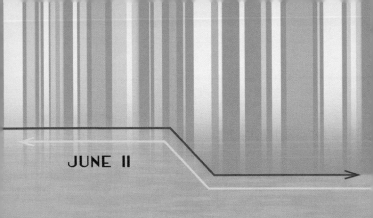

JUNE 11

Many a father wishes he were strong enough to tear a telephone book in two—especially if he has a teenage daughter.

GUY LOMBARDO

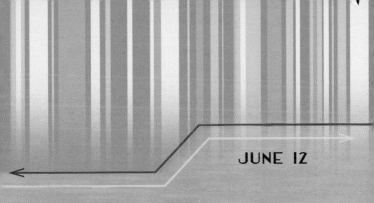

JUNE 12

To acquire knowledge, one must study; but to acquire wisdom, one must observe.

MARILYN VOS SAVANT

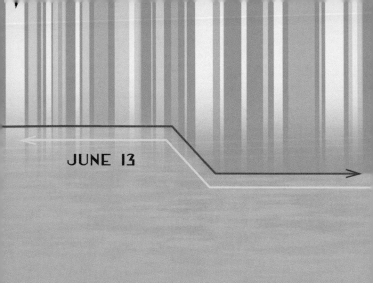

JUNE 13

Every day holds the possibility of a miracle.

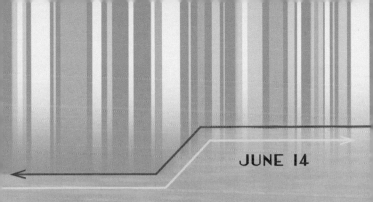

JUNE 14

Prayer moves mountains. It's how we let God into this world. He waits for us to ask Him in, and prayer is how we do that.

GERRID S.

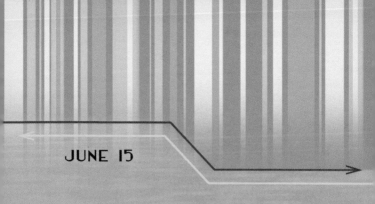

JUNE 15

Be assured that from the first day we heard of you, we haven't stopped praying for you, asking God to give you wise minds and spirits attuned to his will, and so acquire a thorough understanding of the ways in which God works. We pray that you'll live well for the Master, making him proud of you as you work hard in his orchard. As you learn more and more how God works, you will learn how to do *your* work.

COLOSSIANS 1:9-10 THE MESSAGE

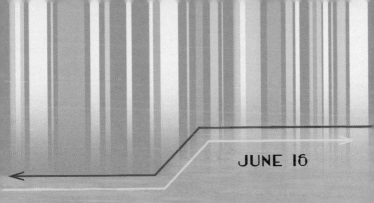

JUNE 16

Give generously, save consistently, and never spend more money than you have.

MARY HUNT

JUNE 17

The most important single ingredient in the formula of success is knowing how to get along with people.

THEODORE ROOSEVELT

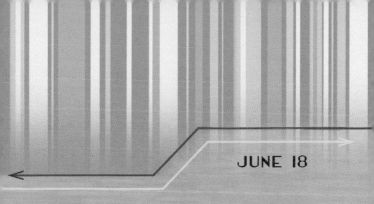

JUNE 18

I am still confident of this: I will see the
goodness of the Lord in the land of the living.
Wait for the Lord; be strong and take heart
and wait for the Lord.

PSALM 27:13-14 NIV

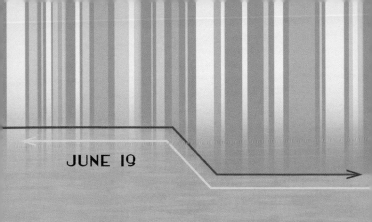

JUNE 19

Just don't give up trying to do what you really want to do. Where there is love and inspiration, I don't think you can go wrong.

ELLA FITZGERALD

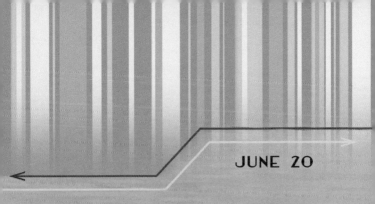

JUNE 20

Each day is a treasure box of gifts from God, just waiting to be opened. Open your gifts with excitement. You will find forgiveness attached to ribbons of joy. You will find love wrapped in sparkling gems.

JOAN CLAYTON

JUNE 21

I've learned that you can get by on charm
for about fifteen minutes. After that, you'd better
know something.

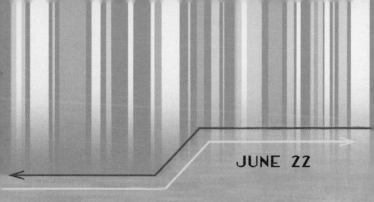

JUNE 22

Can two walk together, except they be agreed?

AMOS 3:3 KJV

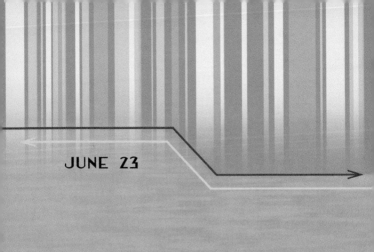

JUNE 23

If what you are doing is questionable
in your mind, quit!

SCOTT H.

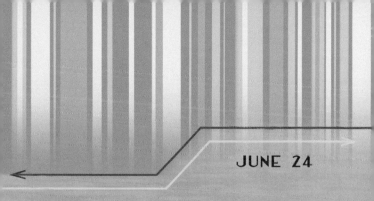

JUNE 24

When you have laboriously accomplished your daily task, go to sleep in peace. God is awake.

VICTOR HUGO

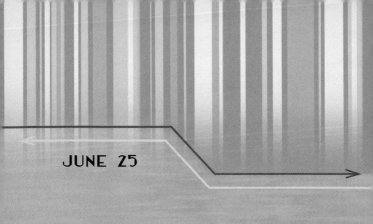

JUNE 25

You pay God a compliment by asking great things of Him.

TERESA OF AVILA

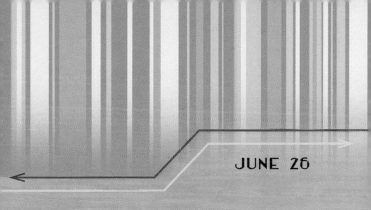

JUNE 26

There is always room for improvement—it's the
biggest room in the house.

LOUISE HEATH LEBER

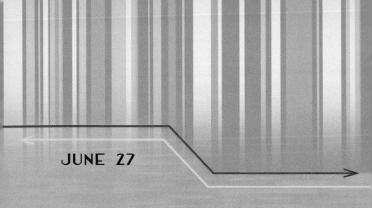

JUNE 27

What will come, will come. You can't spend your life worrying.

RYAN C.

Be anxious for nothing, but in everything by prayer and supplication with thanksgiving let your requests be made known to God.

PHILIPPIANS 4:6 NASB

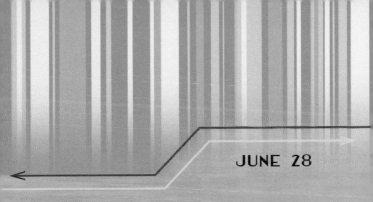

JUNE 28

So go for it.... Don't be afraid of mistakes or defeats; they are the building blocks for all your successes.

BARBARA JOHNSON

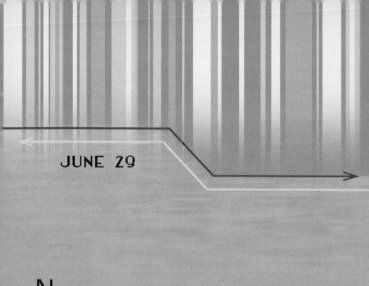

JUNE 29

Never, never, never quit.

WINSTON CHURCHILL

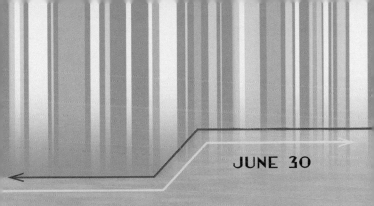

JUNE 30

Know that God is unlimited. He can do anything.

AARON H.

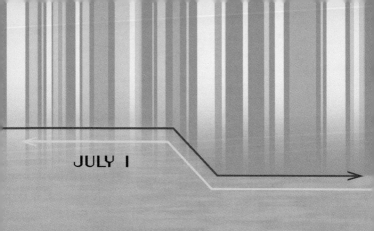

JULY 1

The best thing about the future is that it comes only one day at a time.

ABRAHAM LINCOLN

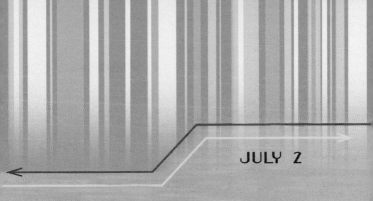

JULY 2

But that does not mean we want to tell you exactly how to put your faith into practice. We want to work together with you so you will be full of joy as you stand firm in your faith.

2 CORINTHIANS 1:24 NLT

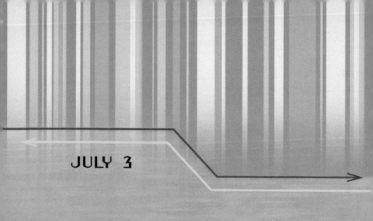

JULY 3

John Wayne called it grit. General Patton called it guts. Vince Lombardi called it "the stuff it takes to be a winner." The Bible calls it endurance.

JOE WHITE

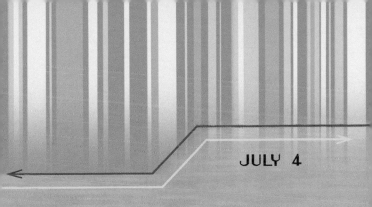

JULY 4

God cares for the world He created, from the
rising of a nation to the falling of the sparrow.

KEN GIRE

JULY 5

Do not follow where the path may lead. Go instead where there is no path and leave a trail.

I opened my eyes only to find
I was back at the place I had begun.
Helpless and broken, I strained and cried out,
"Surely the enemy has won."
But I felt His peace that passes understanding,
Grace that is never ending,
Love that overflows my soul.

SARA GROVES

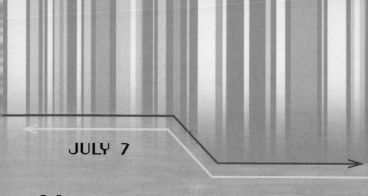

JULY 7

Most kids are excited to be alive—they jump out of bed and believe they can do anything. Unfortunately, a lot of them lose that feeling.

BENJAMIN V.

Dear friend, guard Clear Thinking and Common Sense with your life; don't for a minute lose sight of them. They'll keep your soul alive and well, they'll keep you fit and attractive.

PROVERBS 3:21-22 THE MESSAGE

JULY 8

Give what you have. To someone it may be better than you dare to think.

LONGFELLOW

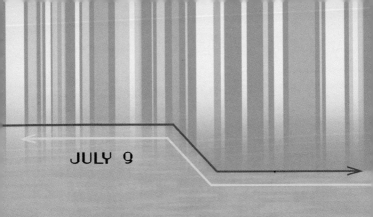

JULY 9

You are you. There is only one you. And you are important.

CHARLES SWINDOLL

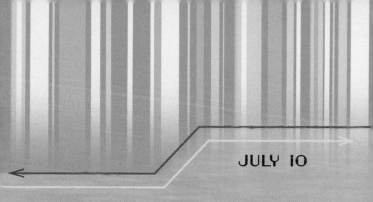

JULY 10

God's gifts put man's best dreams to shame.

ELIZABETH BARRETT BROWNING

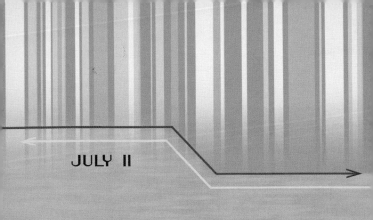

JULY II

When your world falls apart, run to the One who creates worlds.

DREA T.

You are the light of the world. A city on a hill
cannot be hidden. Neither do people light a lamp
and put it under a bowl. Instead they put it on its
stand, and it gives light to everyone in the house.
In the same way, let your light shine before men,
that they may see your good deeds and praise
your Father in heaven.

MATTHEW 5:14-16 NIV

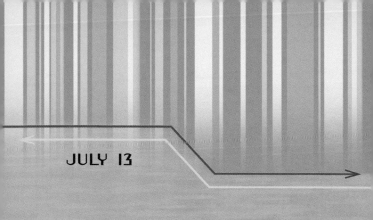

JULY 13

A friend is one who laughs at your jokes when they're not very funny and sympathizes with your problems when they're not very serious.

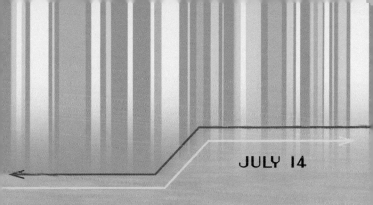

JULY 14

It's the life behind the words that makes the testimony effective.

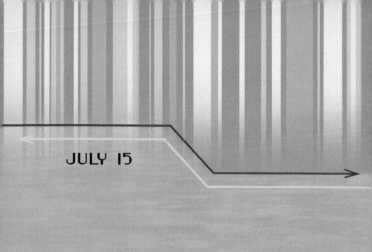

JULY 15

Don't be afraid to go out on a limb—that's where the fruit is.

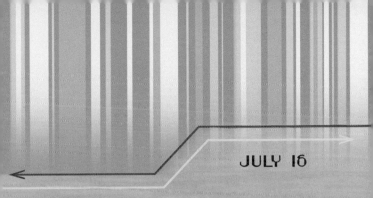

JULY 16

Never forget the nine most important words
of any family—"I love you. You are beautiful.
Please forgive me."

H. JACKSON BROWN JR.

JULY 17

O Lord, you have searched me and you know me. You know when I sit and when I rise; you perceive my thoughts from afar. You discern my going out and my lying down; you are familiar with all my ways. Before a word is on my tongue you know it completely, O Lord. You hem me in— behind and before; you have laid your hand upon me. Such knowledge is too wonderful for me, too lofty for me to attain.

PSALM 139:1-6 NIV

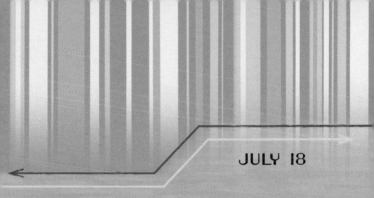

JULY 18

To have a friend is to have one of the sweetest gifts that life can bring; to be a friend is to have a solemn and tender education of soul from day to day.

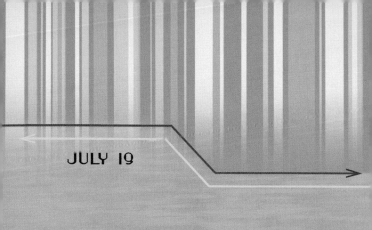

JULY 19

Age does not diminish the extreme disappointment of having a scoop of ice cream fall from the cone.

JIM FIEBIG

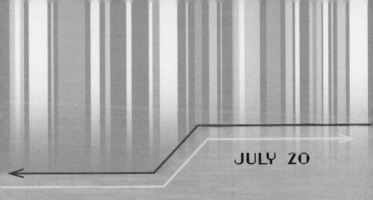

JULY 20

A smile costs nothing but gives much. It takes but a moment, but the memory of it sometimes lasts forever.

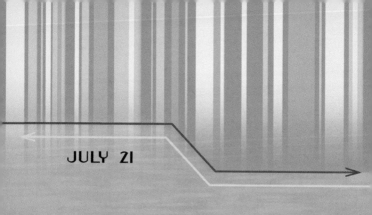

JULY 21

I have learned to choose my friends by their character and my socks by their color.

KYLE SANDBURG

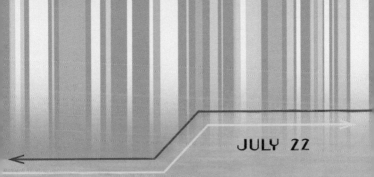

JULY 22

If not me, then who?

SCOTT H.

It is he who saved us and chose us for his holy work not because we deserved it but because that was his plan long before the world began—to show his love and kindness to us through Christ.

2 TIMOTHY 1:9 TLB

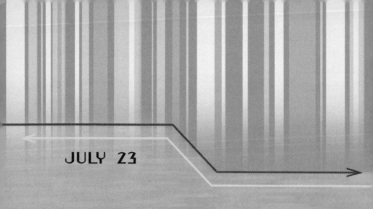

JULY 23

You were put on earth to make a contribution. You weren't created just to consume resources— to eat, breathe, and take up space. God designed you to make a difference with your life.

RICK WARREN

If you're used to winning and find yourself at that place where you've lost, watch for the reward that you never allowed yourself to notice, one that can be so much more satisfying—the real winner's face.

SHAUN SWARTZ

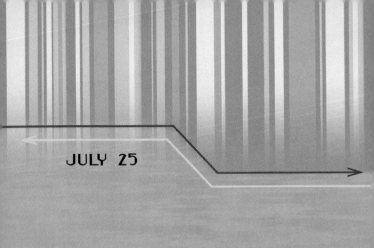

JULY 25

It is never too late to start doing what is right!

CHARLES SWINDOLL

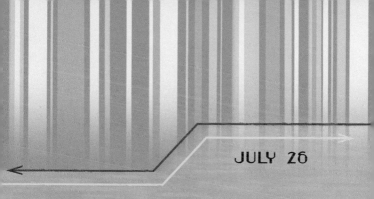

JULY 26

With friends, it doesn't matter what we do, as long as we are together.

CAITLIN S.

JULY 27

For everything that was written in the past was written to teach us, so that through endurance and the encouragement of the Scriptures we might have hope.

ROMANS 15:4 NIV

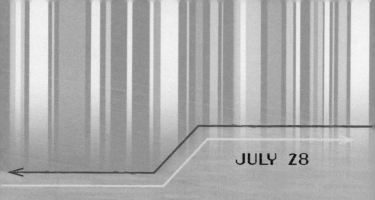

God can't fix a broken heart if you don't give him all the pieces.

JENNIFER LEIGH YOUNGS

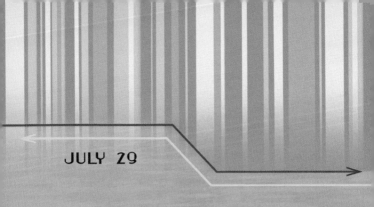

JULY 29

True friendships are lasting because true love is eternal. A friendship in which heart speaks to heart is a gift from God, and no gift that comes from God is temporary or occasional.

HENRI J. M. NOUWEN

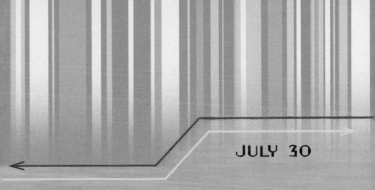

Friends are like newly found diamonds covered in dirt and coal. You will never know their beauty until you have chipped away the cover with tools of love and understanding. Inside, something wonderful but different awaits.

IRENE SOLA'NGE MCCALPHIN

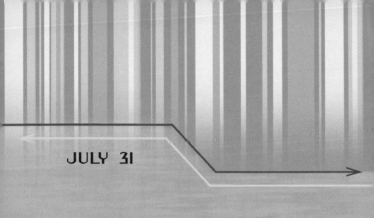

JULY 31

The glory is not in never failing, but in rising
every time you fail.

CHINESE PROVERB

AUGUST 1

Confess your sins to each other and pray for each other so that you may be healed. The earnest prayer of a righteous person has great power and wonderful results.

JAMES 5:16 NLT

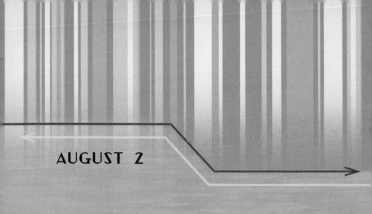

AUGUST 2

It really feels good to do something for somebody else.

GUY RICE DOUD

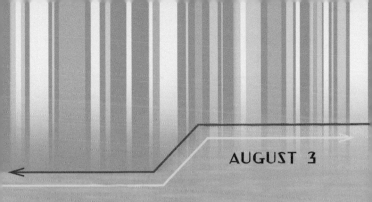

AUGUST 3

Those who remember the past with a clear conscience need have no fear of the future.

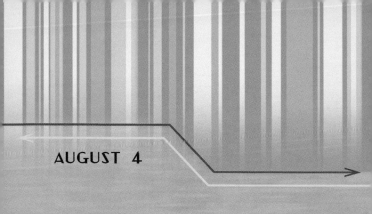

God loves me because of who I am, not because of how I act or who I hang out with. He likes me for me.

JACOB D.

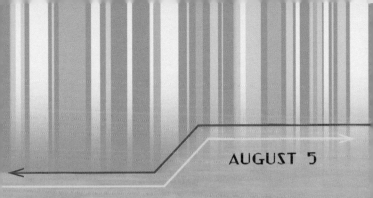

We have a God who delights in impossibilities.

ANDREW MURRAY

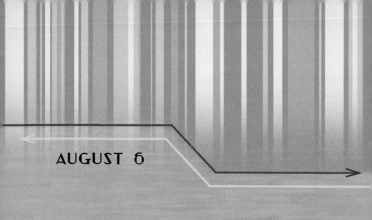

AUGUST 6

God's blessing makes life rich; nothing we do
can improve on God.

PROVERBS 10:22 THE MESSAGE

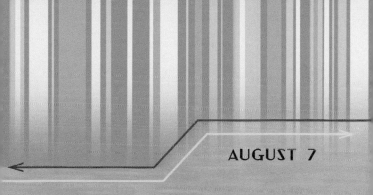

The really great person is the person who makes everyone feel great.

G. K. CHESTERTON

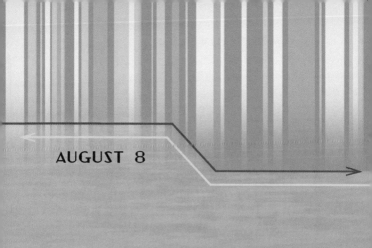

AUGUST 8

Let not the grass grow on the path of friendship.

NATIVE AMERICAN PROVERB

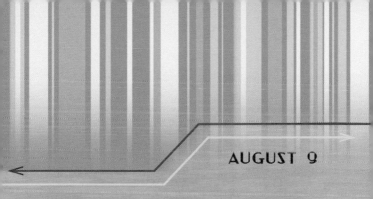

AUGUST 9

We realize that what we are accomplishing is a drop in the ocean. But if this drop were not in the ocean, it would be missed.

MOTHER TERESA

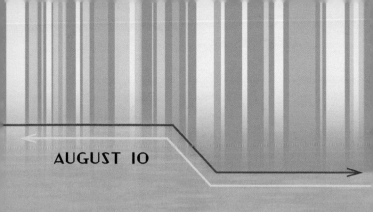

I am working hard
To clean my house and set it straight—
To not let pride get in the way,
To catch an eternal vision of
What I am to become.

SARA GROVES

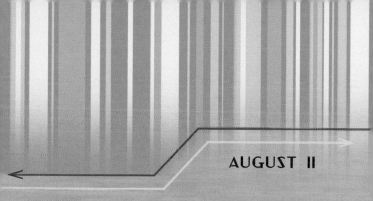

AUGUST 11

Do not be yoked together with unbelievers.
For what do righteousness and wickedness have
in common? Or what fellowship can light have
with darkness?

2 CORINTHIANS 6:14 NIV

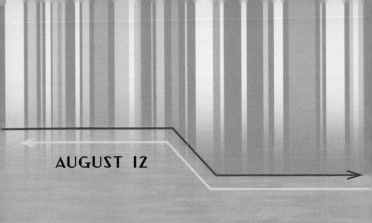

AUGUST 12

Young people often learn more than adults give them credit for.

PAMELA WATERMAN

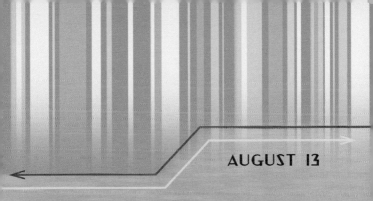

A friend is someone who understands your past, believes in your future, and accepts you today just the way you are.

BEVERLY LAHAYE

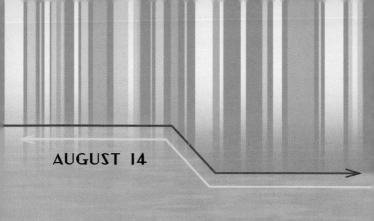

AUGUST 14

God's love is never ending, never ceasing, and with all His heart.

ZACH C.

Don't be afraid,...I have called you by name; you are mine. When you go through deep waters and great trouble, I will be with you. When you go through rivers of difficulty, you will not drown! When you walk through the fire of oppression, you will not be burned up—the flames will not consume you.

ISAIAH 43:1-2 TLB

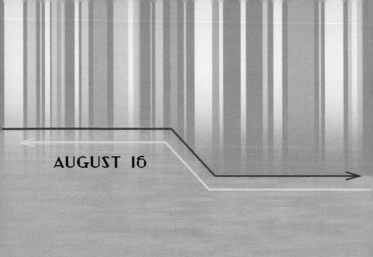

AUGUST 16

You are sowing the flowers of tomorrow in the seeds of today.

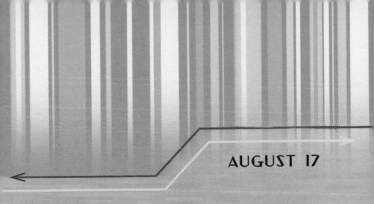

AUGUST 17

How far that little candle throws his beams!
So shines a good deed in a naughty world.

SHAKESPEARE

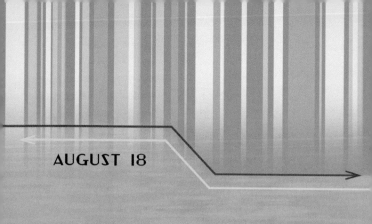

AUGUST 18

Are you aware that the Father takes delight
in you and that He thinks about you all the time?

JACK FROST

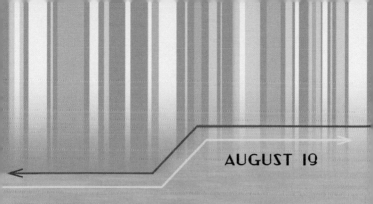

AUGUST 19

Thanks to my family, I've learned that money isn't necessary for true happiness.

RANDI C.

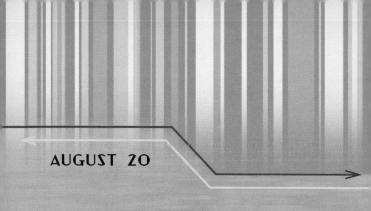

Worry is a waste of time.

NOAH H.

So don't worry about tomorrow, for tomorrow will bring its own worries. Today's trouble is enough for today.

MATTHEW 6:34 NLT

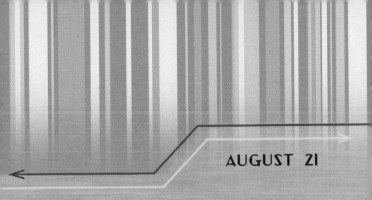

AUGUST 21

Love builds memories that endure, to be treasured up as hints of what shall be hereafter.

BEDE JARRET

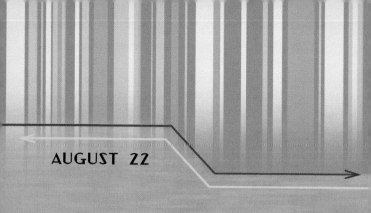

Ⓦhen it is the hardest to trust God—that's the time you should trust Him the most.

LINDSEY S.

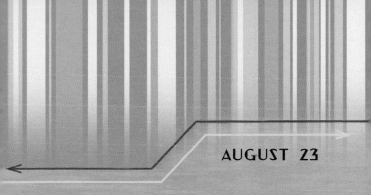

AUGUST 23

Nothing enters your life accidentally—
remember that. Behind our every experience
is our loving, sovereign God.

CHARLES SWINDOLL

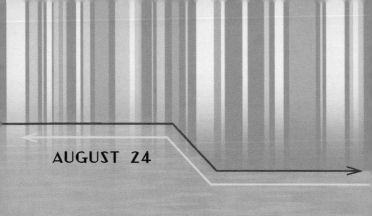

AUGUST 24

Courage doesn't always roar. Sometimes courage
is the little voice at the end of the day that says...
I'll try again tomorrow.

Love is patient, love is kind. It does not envy, it does not boast, it is not proud. It is not rude, it is not self-seeking, it is not easily angered, it keeps no record of wrongs. Love does not delight in evil but rejoices with the truth. It always protects, always trusts, always hopes, always perseveres. Love never fails.

1 CORINTHIANS 13:4-8 NIV

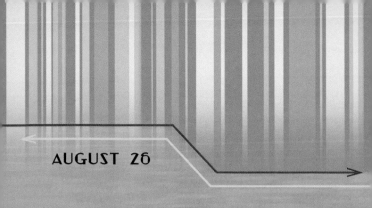

AUGUST 26

A good friend is a connection to life—a tie to the past, a road to the future, the key to sanity in a totally insane world.

LOIS WYSE

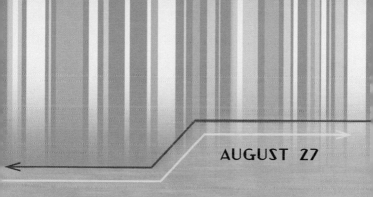

AUGUST 27

You see possibilities in others, but do you ever dream the possibilities within yourself?

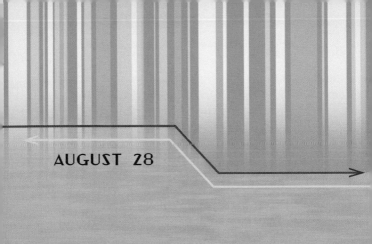

The body is a sacred garment.

MARTHA GRAHAM

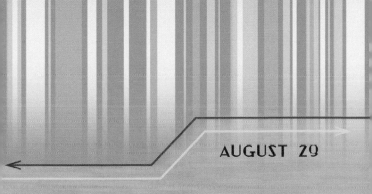

AUGUST 29

How comforting! He knows me completely
and still loves me.

NEVA COYLE

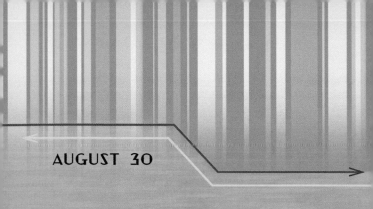

AUGUST 30

Steep yourself in God-reality, God-initiative, God-provisions. You'll find all your everyday human concerns will be met. Don't be afraid of missing out. You're my dearest friends! The Father wants to give you the very kingdom itself.

LUKE 12:31-32 THE MESSAGE

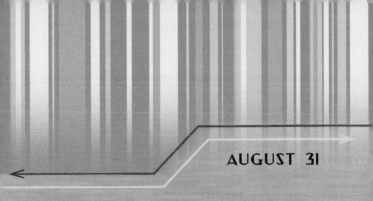

God made me special. No one is like me.

He will never stop loving me for just being me.

KATRINA T.

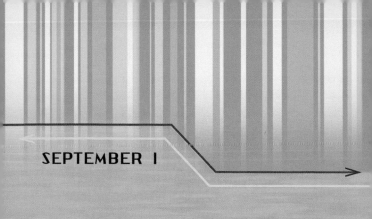

SEPTEMBER 1

Cease to inquire whatever the future has in store,
and take as a gift whatever the day brings forth.

HORACE

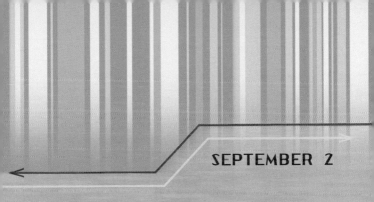

Have confidence that if you have done a little thing well, you can do a bigger thing well too.

WILBUR F. STOREY

SEPTEMBER 3

Grasp the fact that God is for you—let this certainty make its impact on you in relation to what you are up against at this very moment.

J. I. PACKER

All scripture is inspired by God and is useful for teaching, for reproof, for correction, and for training in righteousness, so that everyone who belongs to God may be proficient, equipped for every good work.

2 TIMOTHY 3:16-17 NRSV

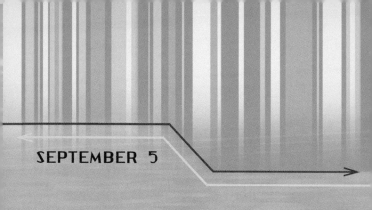

SEPTEMBER 5

God is at work in the world, and He wants you to join Him. This assignment is called your mission. God wants you to have both a ministry in the Body of Christ and a mission in the world.

RICK WARREN

Remember when you were at your best?
Go there again.

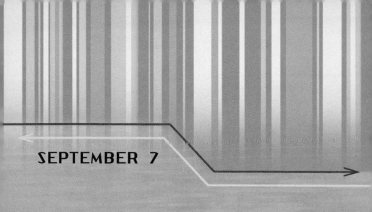

SEPTEMBER 7

Now may the warming love of friends
Surround you as you go
Down the path of light and laughter
Where the happy memories grow.

HELEN LOWRIE MARSHALL

SEPTEMBER 8

I know it is hard sometimes, but pray, pray, pray. Ask God for wisdom and strength to overcome your fears. He's listening.

JULLIAN R.

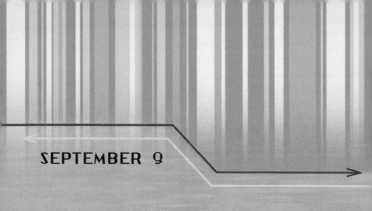

SEPTEMBER 9

If you don't know what you're doing, pray to the Father. He loves to help. You'll get his help, and won't be condescended to when you ask for it. Ask boldly, believingly, without a second thought.

JAMES 1:5-6 THE MESSAGE

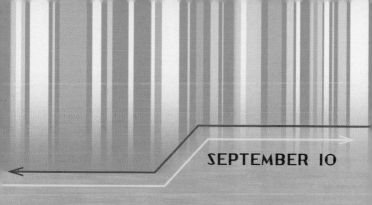

SEPTEMBER 10

The greatest mistake you can make is to be constantly fearful you will make one.

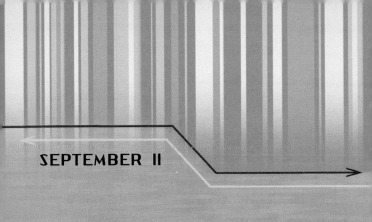

SEPTEMBER 11

The secret of life is that all we have and are is a gift of grace to be shared.

LLOYD JOHN OGILVIE

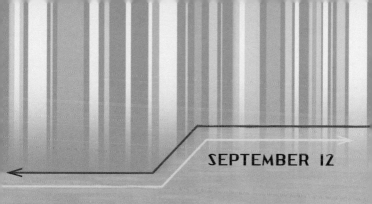

SEPTEMBER 12

I get through bad stuff by asking God to carry me when I can't walk any farther.

SCOTT H.

SEPTEMBER 13

God uses ordinary people to do extraordinary things.

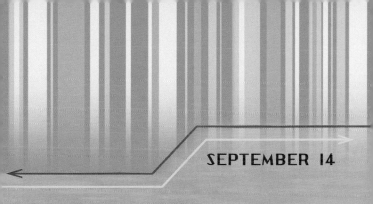

SEPTEMBER 14

This will be your opportunity to tell them about me— yes, to witness to the world.

MATTHEW 10:18 NLT

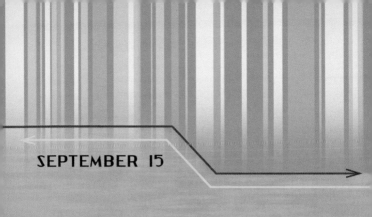

No matter where I am,
This is my joy,
That You specialize in hurt and broken souls
To make me more like Christ.

SARA GROVES

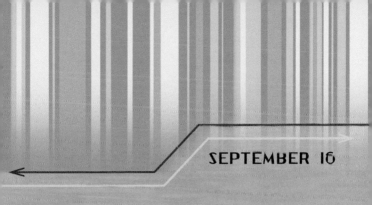

SEPTEMBER 16

Faith makes things possible, not necessarily easy.

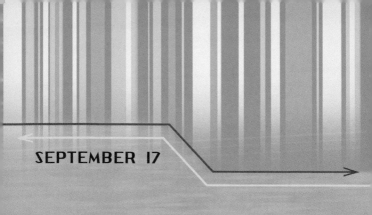

SEPTEMBER 17

God's hand is extended to you—not to push you away, but to draw you close; not to keep you at a distance, but to hold you near to His heart.

ROY LESSIN

It is easier to resist at the beginning than at the end.

SEPTEMBER 19

Is the law, therefore, opposed to the promises of God? Absolutely not! For if a law had been given that could impart life, then righteousness would certainly have come by the law. But the Scripture declares that the whole world is a prisoner of sin, so that what was promised, being given through faith in Jesus Christ, might be given to those who believe.

GALATIANS 3:21-22 NIV

Everything about the way God designed you
is not only perfectly pretty, it's part of His perfect
plan.... You were God's idea.

ANDREA STEPHENS

SEPTEMBER 21

Love is the only force capable of transforming
an enemy into a friend.

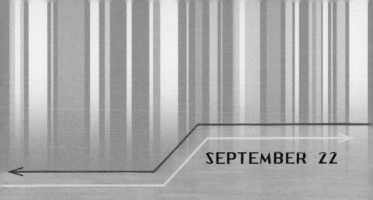

SEPTEMBER 22

Triumph—"umph" added to "try."

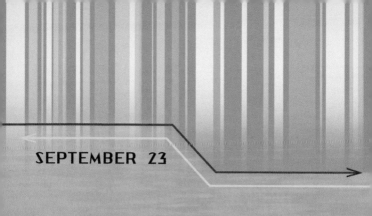

SEPTEMBER 23

Success is going from failure to failure without losing enthusiasm.

WINSTON CHURCHILL

Stand up for what you believe in and stand out of the crowd, be an individual.

KATIE F.

Do you want to stand out? Then step down.
Be a servant. If you puff yourself up, you'll get the
wind knocked out of you. But if you're content
to simply be yourself, your life will count for plenty.

MATTHEW 23:11-12 THE MESSAGE

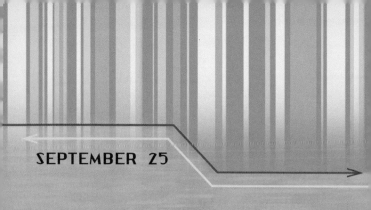

SEPTEMBER 25

If you have built castles in the sky, your work need not be lost; that is where they should be. Now put foundations under them.

HENRY DAVID THOREAU

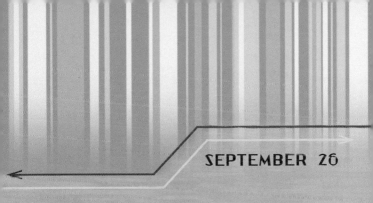

Hold tight rein of the three "t"s—thought, temper, and tongue—and you will have few regrets.

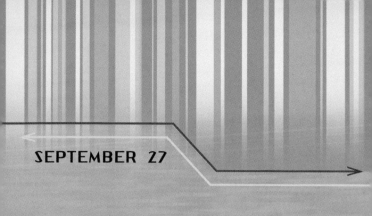

SEPTEMBER 27

No one is useless in this world who lightens the burdens of it for another.

CHARLES DICKENS

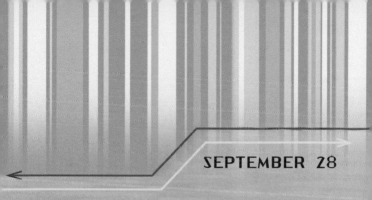

SEPTEMBER 28

Don't let little things become big things.

PATTY R.

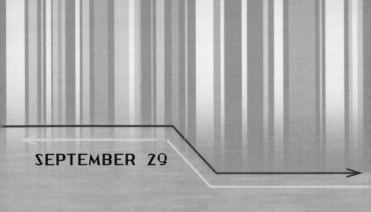

For you will be his witness to all the world of what you have seen and heard. And now why do you delay?

ACTS 22:15-16 NRSV

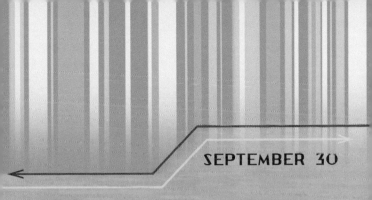

SEPTEMBER 30

Character is what you do when no one is looking.

HENRY HUFFMAN

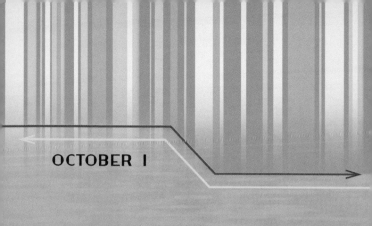

OCTOBER I

There is a past which is gone forever, but there is a future which is still our own.

F. W. ROBERTSON

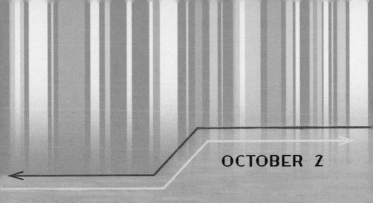

You have the right to say "no" without feeling guilty.

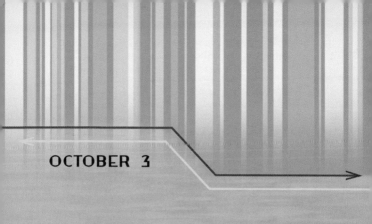

OCTOBER 3

What have we to expect? Anything.
What have we to hope for? Everything.
What have we to fear? Nothing.

EDWARD B. PUSEY

OCTOBER 4

For everything we know about God's Word is summed up in a single sentence: Love others as you love yourself. That's an act of true freedom.

GALATIANS 5:14 THE MESSAGE

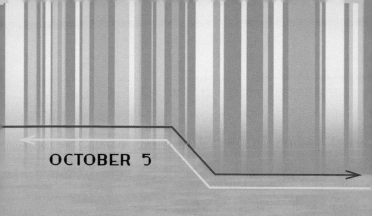

OCTOBER 5

Once you know what God wants you to do,
the blessing comes in actually doing it....
That is what the *purpose-driven* life is all about.
Neither past nor future generations can serve
God's purpose in this generation. Only we can.

RICK WARREN

Character is what emerges from all the little things you were too busy to do yesterday, but did anyway.

MIGNON MCLAUGHLIN

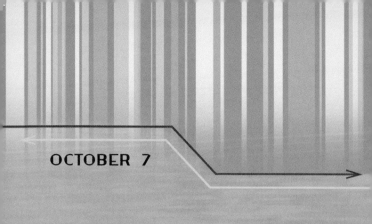

Worry does not empty tomorrow of its sorrow;
it empties today of its strength.

CORRIE TEN BOOM

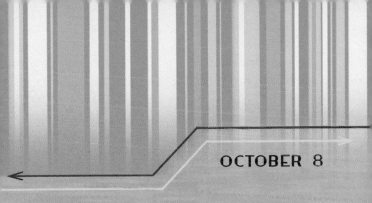

OCTOBER 8

Do not pray for an easy life. Pray to be a strong person.

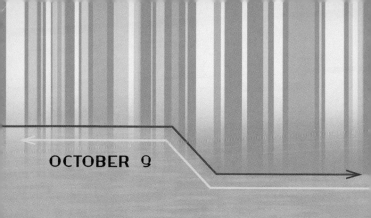

OCTOBER 9

To those who use well what they are given,
even more will be given, and they will have an
abundance. But from those who are unfaithful,
even what little they have will be taken away.

MATTHEW 25:29 NLT

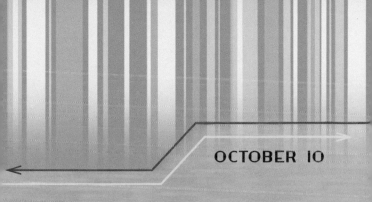

OCTOBER 10

A ship in the harbor is safe, but that is not what ships are built for.

GRACE MURRAY HOPPER

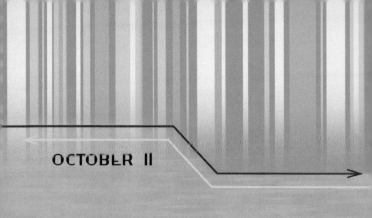

OCTOBER 11

Friendship is a long time in forming, it is of slow growth, through many trials and months of familiarity.

JEAN DE LA BRUYÈRE

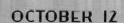

OCTOBER 12

God's bright sunshine overhead,
God's flowers beside your feet...
And by such pleasant pathways led,
May all your life be sweet.

HELEN WAITHMAN

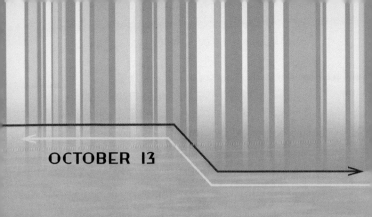

OCTOBER 13

Be a first-rate version of yourself and not a
second-rate version of someone else.

ALLISON S.

In this you greatly rejoice, though now for a little while you may have had to suffer grief in all kinds of trials. These have come so that your faith—of greater worth than gold, which perishes even though refined by fire—may be proved genuine and may result in praise, glory and honor when Jesus Christ is revealed.

1 PETER 1:6-7 NIV

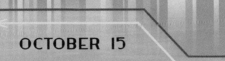

OCTOBER 15

The same person who created the minuscule amoebas and the majestic mountains, the delicate purple orchid and the deep blue ocean, the sun that shines by day and the stars that glow by night. The very same all-wise, all-knowing, all-powerful God, used His special touch to create you.

ANDREA STEPHENS

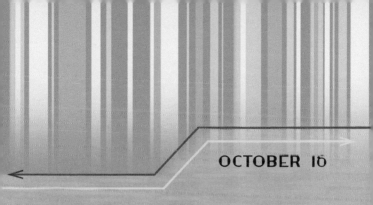

Happiness is found along the way, not at the end of the road.

OCTOBER 17

Perseverance is failing nineteen times and succeeding the twentieth.

J. ANDREWS

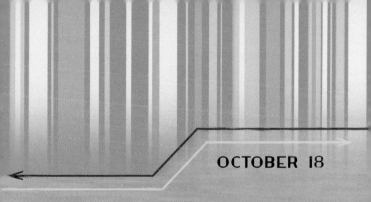

OCTOBER 18

They are well guided that God guides.

SCOTTISH PROVERB

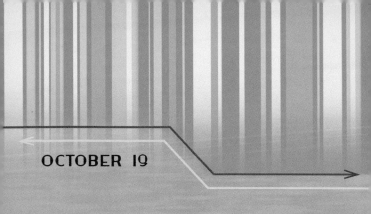

OCTOBER 19

Through the heartfelt mercies of our God,
God's Sunrise will break in upon us, shining
on those in the darkness, those sitting in the
shadow of death, then showing us the way,
one foot at a time, down the path of peace.

LUKE 1:78-79 THE MESSAGE

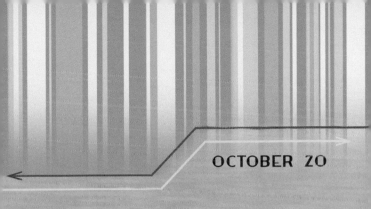

OCTOBER 20

Life is to be fortified by many friendships. To love and be loved is the greatest happiness of existence.

SYDNEY SMITH

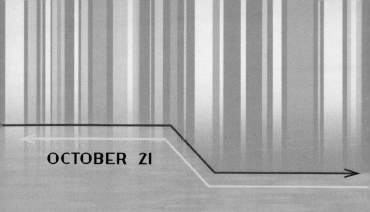

OCTOBER 21

Keep on praying no matter what. You will get answers to whatever you want—the answers may not come in the way you want them to or be exactly what you want the answers to be, but if you keep praying you will get answers.

LIZ S.

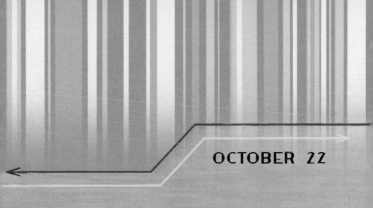

OCTOBER 22

God loves you in the morning sun and the
evening rain, without caution or regret.

BRENNAN MANNING

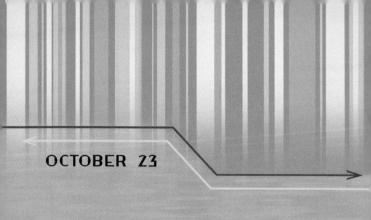

OCTOBER 23

Life isn't about the breaths we take, it's about the moments that take our breath away.

RUTH E. RENKEL

OCTOBER 24

Always be full of joy in the Lord; I say it again, rejoice!

PHILIPPIANS 4:4 TLB

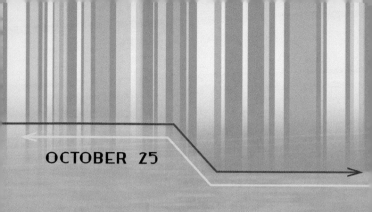

OCTOBER 25

Use what talents you possess: the woods would be very silent if no birds sang there except those that sang best.

HENRY VAN DYKE

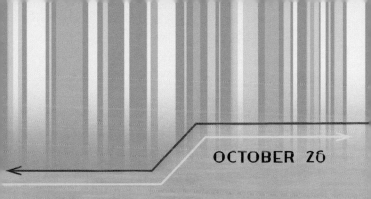

OCTOBER 26

To act is easy; to think is hard.

GOETHE

OCTOBER 27

Go to the effort. Invest the time. Write the letter.
Make the apology. Take the trip. Purchase the gift.
Do it. The seized opportunity renders joy.

MAX LUCADO

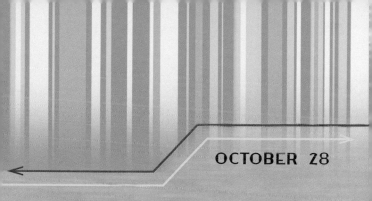

OCTOBER 28

The turning point in the process of growing up is when you discover the core strength within you that survives all hurt.

MAX LERNER

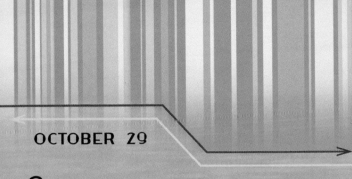

OCTOBER 29

Stay in there. Don't close yourself off from the world. It can't rain all the time.

KRISTIN D.

Though the rain comes in torrents and the floodwaters rise and the winds beat against that house, it won't collapse, because it is built on rock.

MATTHEW 7:25 NLT

Be a living expression of God's kindness.

MOTHER TERESA

OCTOBER 31

Don't let life discourage you; everyone who got where he is had to begin where he was.

RICHARD L. EVANS

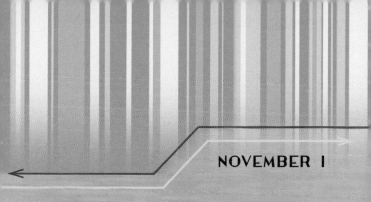

Keep your faith—God will never leave you.
Remember He loves you even when it seems
like no one else does.

EMILY G.

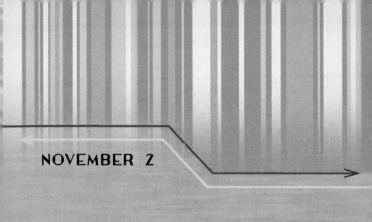

NOVEMBER 2

He who forgives first, wins.

WILLIAM PENN

Ask, and you will be given what you ask for. Seek, and you will find. Knock, and the door will be opened. For everyone who asks, receives. Anyone who seeks, finds. If only you will knock, the door will open.

MATTHEW 7:7-8 TLB

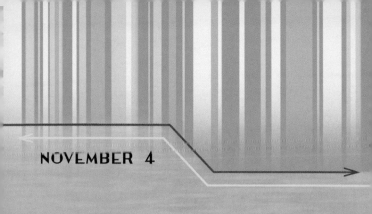

NOVEMBER 4

So remember those things which will help you forward, but forget those things which will only hold you back.

RICHARD C. WOODSOME

A dream is just a dream. A goal is a dream with a plan and a deadline.

HARVEY MACKAY

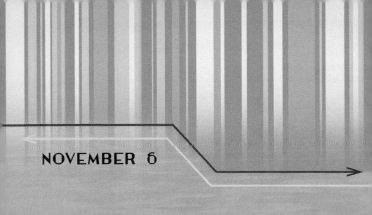

NOVEMBER 6

God...will take care of you day and night forever.

NORMAN VINCENT PEALE

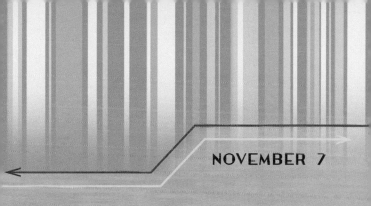

NOVEMBER 7

The need to fit in is a dangerous thing.
Don't give in.

JOHN V.

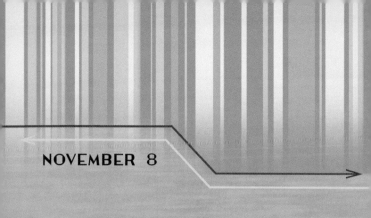

NOVEMBER 8

Run away from sexual sin! No other sin so clearly affects the body as this one does. For sexual immorality is a sin against your own body.

1 CORINTHIANS 6:18 NLT

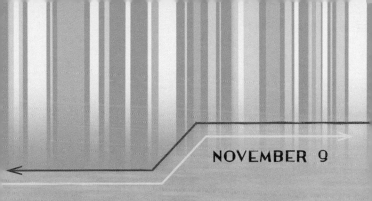

Failures are a normal part of life. They are not disasters that cannot be overcome. A failure means you can try again.

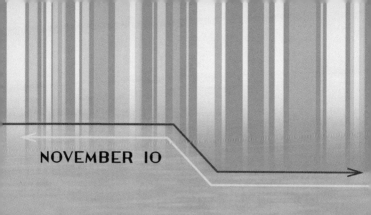

NOVEMBER 10

Good friends are like shock absorbers. They help you take the lumps and bumps on the road of life.

FRANK TYGER

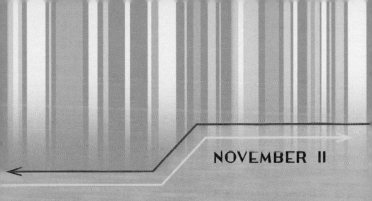

Most dreams take hard work and time.
You need to keep that in mind.

JANNA L. GRABER

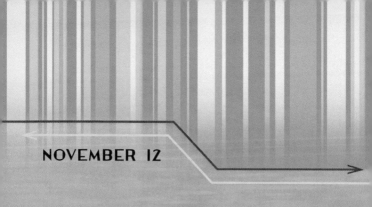

NOVEMBER 12

It is only in God that we discover our origin,
our identity, our meaning, our purpose,
our significance, and our destiny. Every other
path leads to a dead end.

RICK WARREN

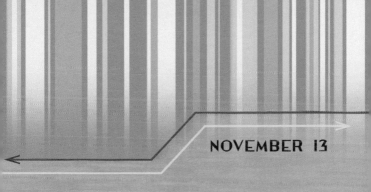

NOVEMBER 13

Honor your father and mother. Then you will live a long, full life in the land the Lord your God will give you.

EXODUS 20:12 NLT

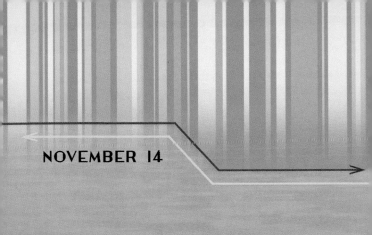

NOVEMBER 14

It takes both the sun and the rain to make a rainbow.

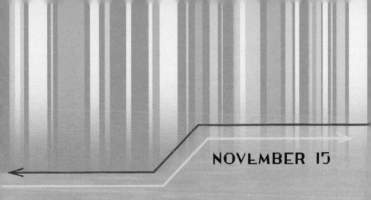

NOVEMBER 15

A word once let out of the cage cannot not be whistled back again

HORACE

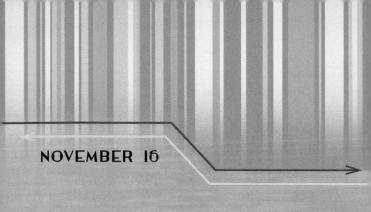

NOVEMBER 16

For all of us, whether we walk old paths or blaze new trails, friends remain important.

LOIS WYSE

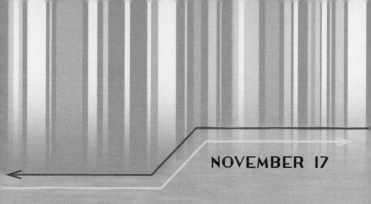

NOVEMBER 17

When we all think alike, no one things
very much.

WALTER LIPPMANN

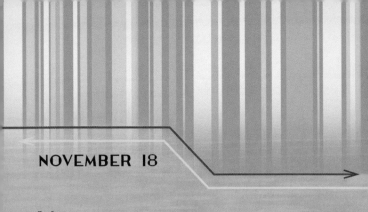

NOVEMBER 18

Never give up. When it feels the worst,
God is there.

AMANDA G.

But in my distress I cried out to the Lord; yes,
I called to my God for help. He heard me from
his sanctuary; my cry reached his ears.

2 SAMUEL 22:7 NLT

We all need friends.

LANNY MCFARLAND

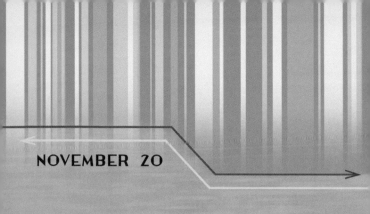

NOVEMBER 20

God is disappointed when you sin. He cries
when bad stuff happens to you. He is overjoyed
to see you succeed. But all He really wants
is to wrap His arms around you and tell you
He loves you.

KARLYNN O.

Friends believe in your dreams as much as you do.

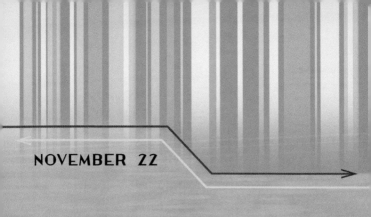

NOVEMBER 22

Live for God and not for things.

HALEY G.

NOVEMBER 23

For surely I know the plans I have for you, says the Lord, plans for your welfare and not for harm, to give you a future with hope.

JEREMIAH 29:11 NRSV

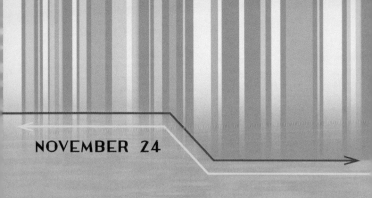

NOVEMBER 24

When one door of happiness closes, another opens; but often we look so long at the closed door that we do not see the one that has been opened for us.

HELEN KELLER

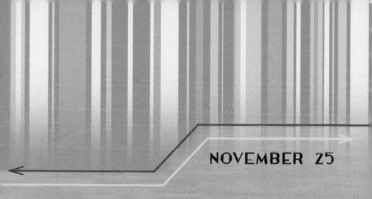

NOVEMBER 25

The best of all is, God with us!

JOHN WESLEY

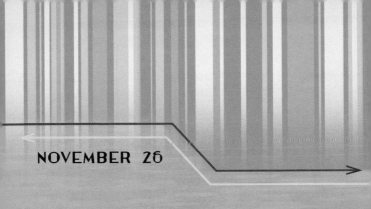

NOVEMBER 26

If you have made mistakes, even serious ones,
there is always another chance for you.
What we call failure is not the falling down,
but the staying down.

MARY PICKFORD

Be a friend; the rest will follow.

EMILY DICKINSON

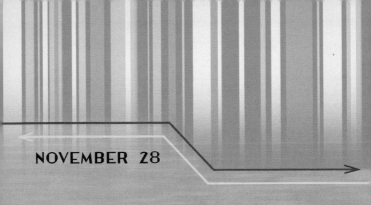

NOVEMBER 28

You will be blessed by the things you pray about.

ADAM B.

That is what is meant by the Scriptures which say that no mere man has ever seen, heard, or even imagined what wonderful things God has ready for those who love the Lord.

1 CORINTHIANS 2:9 TLB

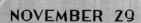

NOVEMBER 29

God wants to give you the strength and skill to climb your troublesome mountain and stand at last triumphant at the top!

GLORIA GAITHER

NOVEMBER 30

Improvement counts no matter how small.

If you need more strength, you will have it, be sure of that.... Your business is with the present; leave the future in His hands who will be sure to do the best, the very best for you.

PRISCILLA MAURICE

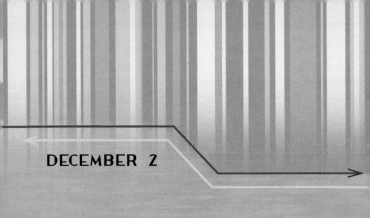

DECEMBER 2

Discovery consists in seeing what everyone else has seen and thinking what no one else has thought.

ALBERT SZENT-GYÖRGYI

Stay away from the love of money; be satisfied with what you have. For God has said, "I will never, never fail you nor forsake you." That is why we can say without any doubt or fear, "The Lord is my Helper, and I am not afraid of anything that mere man can do to me."

HEBREWS 13:5-6 TLB

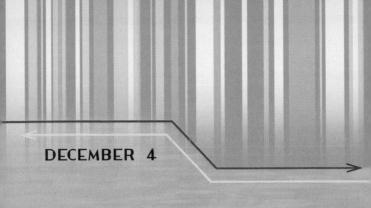

DECEMBER 4

If it can be verified, we don't need faith…. Faith is for that which lies on the other side of reason. Faith is what makes life bearable, with all its tragedies and ambiguities and sudden, startling joys.

MADELEINE L'ENGLE

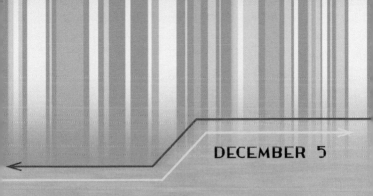

DECEMBER 5

Never fear shadows. They simply mean there's a light shining somewhere nearby.

RUTH E. RENKEL

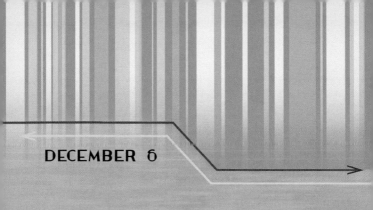

DECEMBER 6

If you really want to be happy, nobody can stop you.

MARY TRICKY

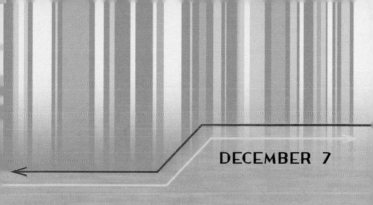

Other people love you, but God loves you so much more!

ALYSSA M.

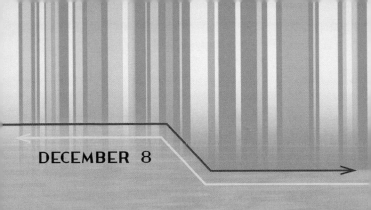

DECEMBER 8

Sometimes a ton of compliments can't make up for one bad criticism.

MAGGIE T.

Worry weighs a person down; an encouraging word cheers a person up.

PROVERBS 12:25 NLT

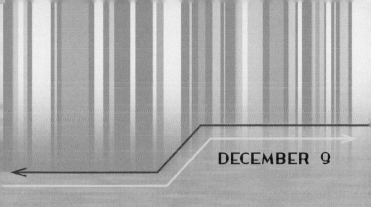

DECEMBER 9

Friends...they cherish one another's hopes.
They are kind to one another's dreams.

HENRY DAVID THOREAU

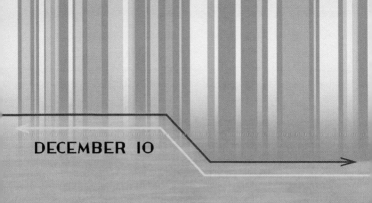

DECEMBER 10

There is no duty we so much underrate as the duty of being happy. By being happy we sow anonymous benefits upon the world.

ROBERT LOUIS STEVENSON

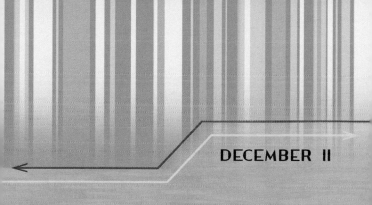

One of Jesus' specialties is to make somebodies out of nobodies.

HENRIETTA MEARS

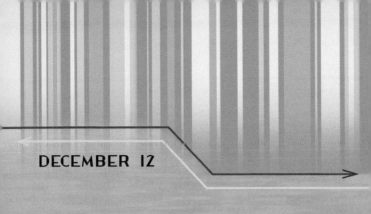

DECEMBER 12

There may be no trumpet sound or loud applause when we make a right decision, just a calm sense of resolution and peace.

GLORIA GAITHER

Not even a sparrow, worth only half a penny, can fall to the ground without your Father knowing it. And the very hairs on your head are all numbered. So don't be afraid; you are more valuable to him than a whole flock of sparrows.

MATTHEW 10:29-31 NLT

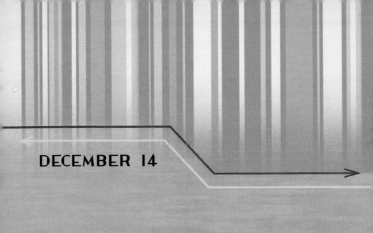

DECEMBER 14

Time has a wonderful way of showing us what really matters.

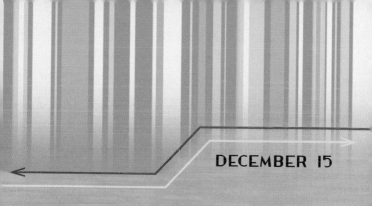

DECEMBER 15

Whatever is good to know is difficult to learn.

GREEK PROVERB

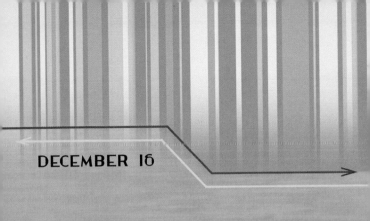

DECEMBER 16

Do not wish to be anything but what you are,
and try to be that perfectly.

FRANCIS DE SALES

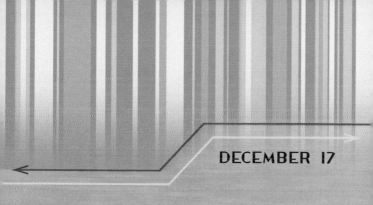

God puts each fresh morning, each new chance of life, into our hands as a gift to see what we will do with it.

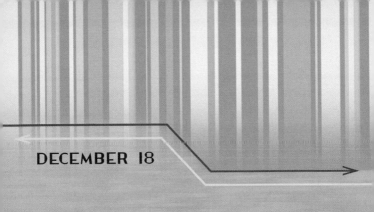

DECEMBER 18

Then I lay down and slept in peace and woke up safely, for the Lord was watching over me. And now, although ten thousand enemies surround me on every side, I am not afraid.

PSALM 3:5-6 TLB

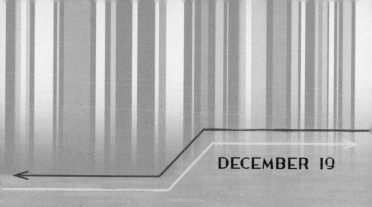

DECEMBER 19

If you pray, you can do amazing things in your life and others' lives.

CASSIE H.

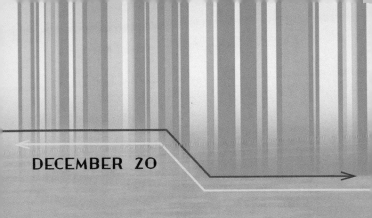

DECEMBER 20

The world is full of friends waiting to meet you.

MARION C. GARRETTY

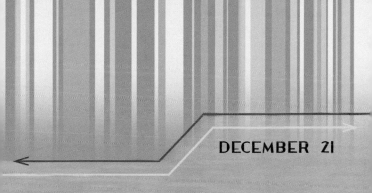

DECEMBER 21

The Lord does not care so much for the
importance of our works as for the love with
which they are done.

TERESA OF AVILA

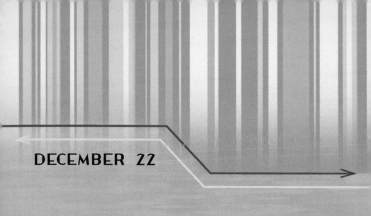

DECEMBER 22

The treasure our heart searches for is found in
the ocean of God's love.

JANET L. WEAVER SMITH

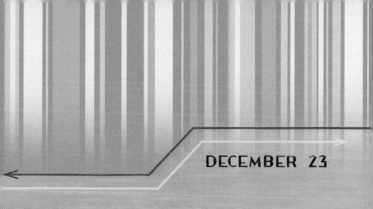

Reading the Bible is important. It's not like you can watch TV and find out more about God.

SARAH M.

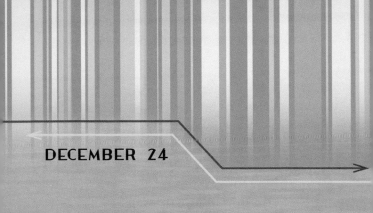

DECEMBER 24

Behold, a virgin shall be with child, and shall bring forth a son, and they shall call his name Emmanuel, which being interpreted is, God with us.

MATTHEW 1:23 KJV

DECEMBER 25

Jesus had been born in a barn, and to a barn the shepherds and the wise men had come, bringing their Christmas gifts.

PEARL S. BUCK

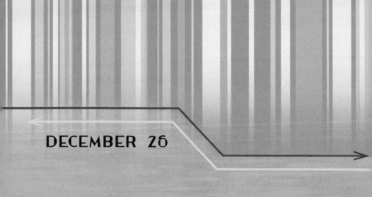

DECEMBER 26

To discover your purpose in life you must turn to God's Word, not the world's wisdom. You must build your life on eternal truths, not pop psychology, success-motivation, or inspirational stories.

RICK WARREN

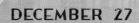

God has created each one of us with great care. He has molded us with His loving hands into the shape that pleases His eye and fills His heart with pride.

ANDREA STEPHENS

DECEMBER 28

We pray that you'll have the strength to stick it out over the long haul—not the grim strength of gritting your teeth but the glory-strength God gives. It is strength that endures the unendurable and spills over into joy, thanking the Father who makes us strong enough to take part in everything bright and beautiful that he has for us.

COLOSSIANS 1:11-12 THE MESSAGE

Everyone has inside himself a piece of good news! The good news is that you really don't know how great you can be, how much you can love, what you can accomplish, and what your potential is.

ANNE FRANK

DECEMBER 30

Today is unique! It has never occurred before and it will never be repeated. At midnight it will end, quietly, suddenly, totally. Forever. But the hours between now and then are opportunities with eternal possibilities.

CHARLES SWINDOLL

The Road goes ever on and on

Down from the door where it began.

Now far ahead the Road has gone,

And I must follow, if I can,

Pursuing it with eager feet,

Until it joins some larger way

Where many paths and errands meet.

And wither then? I cannot say.

J. R. R. TOLKIEN